A Simple Story

Leila Guerriero

A Simple Story
The Last Malambo

Translated from the Spanish
by Frances Riddle

A NEW DIRECTIONS BOOK

A Simple Story was first published in Spanish as *Una historia sencilla.*

Manufactured in the United States of America
New Directions Books are printed on acid-free paper
First published in 2017 as New Directions Paperbook 1365

Library of Congress Cataloging-in-Publication Data
Names: Guerriero, Leila, 1967– author. | Riddle, Frances, translator.
Title: A simple story / by Leila Guerriero ; translated by Frances Riddle.
Other titles: Historia sencilla. English.
Description: New York : New Directions Publishing, 2017.
Identifiers: LCCN 2016039679 | ISBN 9780811226004 (acid-free paper)
Classification: LCC PQ7798.417.U373 H5713 2017 | DDC 863/.7—dc23
LC record available at https://lccn.loc.gov/2016039679

10 9 8 7 6 5 4 3 2 1

New Directions Books are published for James Laughlin
by New Directions Publishing Corporation
80 Eighth Avenue, New York 10011

For Diego,
who always knew,
who never doubted

THIS IS THE STORY of a man who took part in a dance competition.

————————————

The town of Laborde, population six thousand, is located in the southeast of the Córdoba province of Argentina, three hundred miles from Buenos Aires. It was founded in 1903 under the name Las Liebres. The area, colonized by Italian immigrants at the start of the last century, is flush with wheat, corn, and their usual byproducts: flour, and mills that create enough work for hundreds of men and women. The region's prosperity, now sustained by soy, is reflected in towns that look like they were plucked from the imagination of a tidy psychotic child: small urban centers complete with church, main square, town hall, houses with gardens, the latest model four-wheel-drive Toyota Hilux, sometimes two, shiny and new, parked out front. Route 11 passes through many towns like this one: Monte Maíz, Escalante, Pascanas. Between Escalante and Pascanas lies Laborde, a small town with its church, main square, town hall, houses, gardens, trucks, et cetera. It's one more of thousands of towns in the Argentinian interior whose name means nothing to the rest of the country's inhabitants. A town like so many others, in an agricultural region like so many others. But for certain people with a very specific interest, Laborde is an important town. In fact, for these people— with this specific interest—there's no town in the world more important than Laborde.

On Monday, January 5, 2009, the entertainment section of the Argentinian newspaper *La Nación* published an article by the journalist Gabriel Plaza. Titled "The Athletes of Folkloric Dance Are Ready," it took up barely two columns on the front page of the section and two half columns inside, which included the lines: "Considered an elite corps within folkloric dance, the champions walk the streets of Laborde with the same respect proffered to the athletic heroes of Ancient Greece." I saved the article for a few weeks, which turned into months, and then two long years. I had never heard of Laborde but after reading that dramatic description—*elite corps, champions,* and *athletic heroes*—in relation to folkloric dance and an anonymous town in the pampas, I couldn't stop thinking. About what? About going to see it, I guess.

Gaucho, as defined in Felix and Susana Coluccio's *Argentinian Folkloric Dictionary*, is the word used in the River Plate region of Argentina and Uruguay for the horseback riders of the plains or pampas, dedicated to raising livestock. Typically horseback riders and cattle ranchers, known for their skill, pride, and a reserved, melancholic nature. Almost all of their tasks are carried out on horseback, the horse being their constant companion and primary source of wealth. The gaucho stereotype bestows other characteristics: he is considered brave, loyal, strong, indomitable, austere, tough, taciturn, arrogant, fierce, solitary, and nomadic.

Malambo, according to the Argentinian writer and nineteenth-century folklore specialist Ventura Lynch, "is a battle between men who tap in turn to music." It is a dance accompanied by guitar and bass drum, performed by gauchos as a competition of endurance and skill. When Gabriel Plaza spoke of "an elite corps within folkloric dance" this is what he was referring to: the malambo and those who dance it.

The malambo's origins are unclear but it's generally agreed that it came to Argentina by way of Peru. The dance is composed of "a combination of movements and rhythmic taps that are executed with the feet. Each group of movements within a determined musical rhythm is called a figure," writes the Argentinian folkloric dance specialist Héctor Aricó in *Traditional Dances of Argentina*. The movements are composed of sole taps, toe taps, heel taps, jumps, half toe rests, and ankle flexes (impossible contortions). A professional malambo includes more than twenty figures, separated by taps—eight in one and a half seconds—that require enormous muscle strength, incredible reflexes. Every figure carried out by one foot must be executed identically with the opposite foot. This means that a malambo dancer needs to be precise, strong, fast, and elegant with the right foot and precise, strong, fast, and elegant with the left as well.

The malambo has two styles—southern, from the central and southern provinces of Argentina, and northern. The southern style has gentler movements and is accompanied by guitar. The northern style is more forceful and is accompanied by guitar and bass drum. The attire is distinct in each case. For the southern style, the gaucho wears a bowler hat or top hat, white shirt, tie, vest, and a short jacket. An embroidered poncho (called a *chiripá*) is worn over the *cribo* (wide white pants, bordered with embroidery and fringe) tied at the waist by a sash, and a *rastra* (a wide belt with silver or metal decorations). The gaucho's horsehide boot is more like a very thin leather sheath tied carefully at the calf. It covers only the back part of the foot, which hits the floor almost naked. For the northern style, the gaucho wears a shirt, scarf, jacket, *bombachas* (wide pleated pants), and tall leather boots.

This is strictly a masculine dance, which began as a rustic challenge, then hit the twentieth century as a choreographed competition, between two and five minutes long. The malambo's most popular versions, in the shows for export, include dancers that juggle knives or jump over lit candles. In some Argentinian folkloric festivals, only more authentic versions of the dance are permitted. But it's in Laborde, a small town on the flat Argentinian pampas, where the malambo conserves its purest form. Every year since 1966, a prestigious and formidable dance competition is held here. It lasts six days and requires of its participants an intense training, yielding a winner who, like a bull, like a purebred animal, receives the title of champion.

Organized by a group called Friends of the Arts, the National Malambo Festival of Laborde was held for the first time in 1966. In 1973, a committee organized by locals, and made up of manicurists, speech therapists, teachers, business owners, bakers, and homemakers purchased the ten-thousand-square-foot exhibition grounds from the Spanish Society and constructed a stage. That year they drew two thousand spectators. There are now more than six thousand annual attendees and although malambo dominates, additional categories include solo vocalist, instrumental group, dance duo, and regional dance quartet. Outside the competition, prestigious musicians and folkloric groups perform (such as Chango Spasiuk, Peteco Carabajal, or La Callejera). Each year, teams of dancers arrive from all over Argentina and neighboring countries such as Bolivia, Chile, and Paraguay. Residents rent out their homes and local schools are used to accommodate the overflowing crowds. Participation in the festival is not extemporaneous: a nationwide preselection is held months in advance. Only the best make it to Laborde, accompanied by a representative from their province.

The organizing committee is self-financed and they refuse to enter the circuit of the large national folkloric festivals (Cosquín, Jesús María), tsunamis of tradition, televised for the entire country. At Laborde, there is no interest in putting on a visually attractive spectacle. The daily competition schedule, from seven p.m. to six a.m., as well as the intricate dance moves, are not meant for eyes that seek mere entertainment. In Laborde, you won't see gauchos leaping over flames, suits plastered with glitter, or shoes encrusted with rhinestones. If the Laborde competition calls itself "the most Argentinian of festivals" it's because tradition, pure and simple, is the main attraction. The rules prohibit any kind of innovation and what the judges (made up of former champions and specialists) want to see is folklore without the remix: clothes and shoes that respect the modest elegance of the gauchos and *paisanas* (provincial women), acoustic instruments, dance steps that correspond to the province they represent. Piercings, rings, watches, excessive cleavage, and tattoos are prohibited onstage. As the regulations establish: "Rigid or hard boots should be of traditional colors with a half sole. Horsehide leather boots should be authentic, made of traditional material (horsehide, mountain-lion hide). Daggers, *boleadoras*, spears, spurs, or any other element foreign to the dance are not permitted, the musical accompaniment must be traditional in every way, consisting of no more than two instruments, one of which must be guitar. The presentation should not become sensationalist." The uncompromising spirit and faithfulness to tradition is probably what makes this the least-known festival in Argentina. In February 2007, the journalist Laura Falcoff of the newspaper *Clarín* wrote: "Last January the National Malambo Festival celebrated forty years in Laborde, in the province of Córdoba, an almost secret encounter if measured by its faint repercussion in the mass media. For malambo dancers nationwide, on the other hand, Laborde is a true mecca, the geographic center where every year their highest hopes are set." Although it is held in early January, between a Tuesday and the following Monday at dawn, the National Malambo Festival of Laborde is almost never mentioned in the numerous articles about the folkloric festivals that populate the Argentinian summer.

The malambo division of the competition is divided into two categories: quartets (four men tapping in perfect synchronicity) and soloists. These two categories are further divided into subcategories—children's, junior, youth, special youth, and veteran—depending on the age of the participants. But the jewel in the crown is the main malambo soloist category, reserved for men over twenty years old. No more than five competitors (called hopefuls) present per day. For their first performance, taken in turns starting at one a.m., each dances their "strong" malambo, which corresponds to the province they're from: northern style if they're from the north of the country, southern if they're from the south. Afterward, in time slots that begin at three a.m., they dance the "return," the opposite style of the malambo they danced in the first round: those who danced northern, dance southern, and vice versa. Sunday at midday the judges deliberate. They determine which dancers will move on to the finals and communicate their choices to the delegates of each province, who in turn notify the hopefuls. Monday at dawn the selected dancers, between three and five, dance their strong style for a final shot at glory. Around five thirty a.m., with the day brightening and the seats still full, the results of all categories are announced. The final name pronounced is that of the champion, a man whose career in dance is over the moment he receives his crowning glory.

———————

Route 11 is a narrow ribbon of asphalt dotted with rusty railway bridges over which trains no longer pass. During summer in the Southern Hemisphere, January or February, it's the perfect postcard of the humid pampas: fields bursting with shades of green—very, very bright green wheat, green corn. It's Thursday, January 13, 2011, and the entrance to Laborde couldn't be more conspicuous. A mural of the blue-and-white Argentinian flag is captioned LABORDE, NATIONAL MALAMBO CAPITAL. The town has clear limits: seven blocks long and fourteen blocks wide. That's it, and since it's so small, the locals hardly know the street names and instead give directions using landmarks such as "across from the López house" or "next to the ice cream parlor." The exhibition grounds where the National Malambo Festival takes place are simply "the field." At four p.m., under a dry brightness like a dome of flaking plaster, the field hosts the only movement in Laborde. Everything else is closed: houses, kiosks, clothing stores, green grocers, supermarkets, restaurants, cybercafés, shops, rotisseries, the church, the town hall, the community center, the police and fire stations. It's as if Laborde has been paralyzed, or undergone a mummification process. The first thing that comes to mind when I see the squat houses with their cement benches out front, the unchained bicycles leaning against the trees, the cars unlocked with the windows down, is that I've seen hundreds of towns just like this, and that at first glance, there is nothing special about this one.

———————————

Although there are other festivals in Argentina where the malambo is an area of competition (the Cosquín Festival, the Sierra Festival), Laborde, where this dance is the exclusive protagonist, has a rule that makes it unique: the main malambo category is danced for up to five minutes. At other festivals, the accepted time is two and a half to three minutes.

Five minutes is nothing. A minuscule portion of a twelve-hour flight, a mere sigh in a three-day marathon. But everything changes if the correct comparisons are made. The world's fastest runners of the hundred-meter sprint have times under ten seconds. Usain Bolt's record is 9.58 seconds. A malambo dancer reaches a speed similar to that of a sprinter, but they must sustain it for five minutes, not nine seconds. This means that in the year prior to the Laborde competition a malambo dancer receives not only the artistic training of a dancer but also the physical and psychological preparation of an athlete. They don't smoke, drink, or stay up late. They run and go to the gym. They practice concentration, attitude, confidence, and self-esteem. Although there are those who train alone, most have a coach, usually a previous champion. Hopefuls must pay for their classes as well as their coach's trips to the city where they live. Added to this are monthly gym fees, visits to nutritionists and sports doctors, healthy food. The attire can cost between $600 and $800 for each style. The boots for the northern malambo alone cost $140, and they must be replaced every four to six months because they get destroyed. The stay in Laborde is not a minor expense: hopefuls arrive before the start of the festival and spend a total of two weeks there. Almost all hopefuls come from very humble families of homemakers, municipal employees, steel-mill workers, police officers. The most fortunate give classes in schools and dance institutes, but there are also electricians, construction workers, mechanics. Some enter and win the first time, but almost all have to keep trying.

The prize doesn't consist of money, a house or a car, or even a trip. It's a simple trophy made by a local artisan. But the true prize at Laborde, the prize everyone aims for, is unseen: prestige, reverence, recognition, and respect—the glory and honor of being the best among the very few capable of dancing this murderous dance. In the small pantheon of folkloric dancers, a champion at Laborde is an eternal demigod.

But there's something more. In order to preserve the festival's integrity and reaffirm its position as the most prestigious competition, the champions at Laborde have maintained, since 1966, a tacit agreement that although they might dance in other categories, they will never again compete, in this festival or any other, as a main malambo soloist. Breaking this unwritten rule means being shunned by peers. The malambo with which a man wins is also one of the last malambos of his life: becoming champion at Laborde is both the apex of a career and the finale.

In January 2011, I went to this town with a simple idea: to tell the story of a festival and to try to understand why people would want to do such a thing: rise to greatness only to immediately give it up.

———————

On the dirt roads that surround the exhibition grounds there are dozens of stalls that at night sell crafts, T-shirts, CDs. At this time of the afternoon, they are covered with orange tarps that vibrate in the heat and throw off a gelatinous glare. The field is enclosed by a chain-link fence, and upon entering, to the right, is the Gallery of Champions with photos of everyone who has won since 1966. There are also food stands, now closed, that sell empanadas, pizza, *locro* (traditional stew), and grilled meats. On the other side are the bathrooms and the pressroom, a wide square construction with chairs, computers, and a wall covered by a long mirror. At the end of the field, the stage. I've heard stories about this stage. It's said that due to the reverence it commands, many hopefuls have surrendered minutes before going onstage, that a slight downward slope makes it frightening and dangerous, that it's haunted by the terrifying ghosts of the great malambo dancers. What I see is a blue curtain bordered by posters of the festival's sponsors: Finpro Cereals, Cartucho SA Transportation, Casa Roldani Home Goods. Microphones on the ground below amplify each step with cruel precision. In front of the stage, hundreds of plastic chairs, empty. At four thirty p.m. it is difficult to imagine that at some point there will be anything more than what is here now: an island of plastic battered by rolling waves of heat.

I'm studying a eucalyptus canopy that fails to protect me from the sun's claws, when I hear it. A full gallop. Or a machine gun. I turn around to see a man onstage. He wears a beard, top hat, red vest, blue jacket, a bright white *cribo*, a beige *chiripá*, and he rehearses the malambo that he will dance tonight. At first the movement of his legs is not slow but it's human: a speed that you can follow. Then the rhythm speeds up, and speeds up again, and keeps on speeding up, until finally the man stamps one foot on the floor, stares off into the horizon, ecstatic, lowers his head, and begins to breathe like a fish out of water.

"Good," says the guitar player next to him.

———————

Why would a town of sedentary immigrants, orderly and conservative, host a festival that revolves around the most emblematic dance of the gauchos, a nomadic, rebellious people who rejected authority? I don't know. But the National

Malambo Festival of Laborde is like any world championship of any sport: it is a contest of unequaled quality, and those who win are crowned as the world's best. The definitions accepted by the Spanish Royal Academy for the word champion are "a person who obtains primacy in a championship; a person who strives to defend a cause or doctrine; a famous hero in arms; a man who claimed territory and entered into battle in the ancient challenges." The main prize at Laborde seems to encompass them all.

By six p.m. everything has changed. The bars are open, and improvised dance or guitar-strumming sessions convene on street corners. The crowd is young, and although they wear baggy pants, miniskirts, or T-shirts with rock-band logos, there are details that do not belong to their generation or even to the present day: men with long hair and bulky beards, like gauchos, or their stereotype; women with their hair tied back in neat braids, like prudent *paisanas,* or their stereotype.

At eight p.m. the streets that lead to the field are closed to traffic. Inside the exhibition grounds, a tide of people browse the market set up to sell *alfajor* cookies, homemade jams, dried pasta, shower curtains, dog clothes, leather belts, maté gourds, silver jewelry, knives, shirts. The food stalls dispatch plate after plate of stew, pizza, grilled meat. The white chairs fill up as the first categories begin to compete onstage. The children's malambo quartets are dancing now: kids up to nine years old, tiny gauchos who elicit either applause or indifference from the audience without concessions for their age.

Ariel Ávalos sits in a room used as a library. He won the championship in 2000 for the Santa Fe province and he's a rarity: he has very short hair and only a slight beard.

"The regulations don't prohibit you from competing in another festival, but there's an unspoken agreement among the champions. There's no other festival as important as this one and it takes years to prepare, so you have to assign a certain value to all that effort. And the way to make it valuable is by not competing anywhere else. It's a way of saying that there is nothing else equal to it in terms of prestige and importance."

Ávalos is the son of a tile-factory worker and a homemaker. He started dancing at eight in a school dance class, and in 1996 he began to prepare to compete at Laborde. The year he won, he trained with Víctor Cortez—the 1987 champion—and he also saw a sports medicine specialist and a nutritionist. To pay for all this on the salary he earned as an auto mechanic, he had to drop out of college, where he was studying anthropology.

"College will always be there, but the chance to win at Laborde won't. You come here for the honor, not the money. But when you dance there's not a single corner of your body that doesn't boil. What you feel is fire. The city I'm from, San Lorenzo, is on the river. I would go to the riverbank and dance looking at the river. The power of the river is what I feel as I dance. The first obstacle that a malambo dancer has to face is fear. Am I going to finish the malambo well, am I going to run out of breath, out of endurance? When I was preparing myself, a guy who studied psychology gave me an exercise that consisted of standing in front of a mirror and saying: 'I'm the champion.' And you don't stop repeating it until you believe it. I started with the bathroom mirror: 'I'm the champion, I'm the champion.' At first it made me laugh. But then one day I was suddenly convinced. Another thing I did was imagine the voice of the presenter announcing my name—I'd get goose bumps. Even now, when I see the kids dancing, I want to be in their place. I can't even believe there are people who don't dance malambo. But the preparation is very demanding. You need the same ability and efficiency as a top professional soccer player, but no soccer player runs at full speed for five minutes. They run a hundred yards and stop. Only the malambo dancer endures five full minutes. It's brutal. After a minute and a half of malambo your quadriceps start to burn, your breathing changes. If you're not prepared you have to stop."

"Why?" I ask.

"Because you'll suffocate."

Ariel Ávalos was a finalist in the 1998 competition and runner-up (the only other title given in the main malambo category) in 1999. The runner-up is the favorite for the following year's competition. After training even more rigorously, he returned to Laborde on January 3, 2000. A few days earlier, his grandfather started having back pains. Ávalos had been raised by his grandfather from the age of thirteen because his parents' house was very small, and with two other siblings there wasn't enough room for everyone at home. But in the days following his arrival in Laborde, every time he called his family they told him that his grandfather wasn't home, that the doctor had ordered him to walk more and so he had gone out for a stroll. Ariel danced, as the runners-up always do, on the opening night of the competition, and he moved on to the finals. Monday at dawn he descended the stage euphoric: he knew he'd danced well. He was in the dressing room, recovering, when his coach told him what everyone already knew but him: his grandfather was in critical condition, hospitalized, and he and his parents had decided not to tell Ariel out of fear that he'd want to quit the competition. Ariel Ávalos didn't get angry: he understood that things had to be done that way. At five a.m. on Monday, January 17, the presenter announced the name of the champion: it was his. Grateful, he danced a few figures—as the newly crowned champion always does—said a few words, left the stage, ran to his car, and drove back to San Lorenzo. But his grandfather died at eight a.m., while Ariel was still on the road.

"My aunt was the last person to talk to him before he went into the coma," he recalls. "She said, 'Before he went to sleep he asked for you, he asked how it went.' That was the last thing he asked."

Outside, it starts to rain. But through the half-open door I can see that the audience stays in their seats.

Ávalos says, "A malambo dancer has to be willing to sacrifice inconceivable things."

———————

By eleven p.m. it's no longer raining. A provincial delegation dances onstage, and in the aisles, average-looking men and women wearing jeans, skirts, shorts, but also *boinas* and ponchos, are dancing and waving handkerchiefs in the air. It's not a shuffling hodgepodge of amateurs but a concentric flourish of professionals and aficionados. The audience is the pride and joy of Laborde: people who know what they're watching and are capable of judging quality or the lack thereof. For them, Laborde is not a museum of dried-up tradition but a sublime sampling of the culture they were raised with and continue to live in.

Backstage, in a space with cement floors and cinderblock walls, are the dressing rooms. Four of them look like monastic cells with metal doors and a cement counter. The fifth is in a corner. Its walls don't reach the ceiling, and there is no table and no light source. There are two bathrooms with doors that don't close, and a large mirror set into one of the walls. The space— permeated by the spicy smell of anti-inflammatory muscle cream—is constantly full of people dressing and undressing, putting on makeup, stretching, spraying hair spray, braiding braids, fluffing beards, getting nervous, waiting. There are dresses and gaucho attire on hangers, men in underwear, women removing bras with juggling acts of modesty. Before they go onstage, dozens of people warm up their muscles as adrenaline pumps streams of electricity through their pounding hearts.

"No, *boluda,* I can't get the ring off. I wanna die."

A girl in flawless braids and a dress stamped with a sweet flowered pattern is struggling with a huge fuchsia ring. Her finger is swollen and she has only five minutes before she goes onstage. If the judges sees the ring, the entire team risks disqualification.

"Did you try soap?"

"Yes!"

"And spit? Detergent?"

"Yes, yes, and it won't come off!"

"How stupid."

A young man sitting on a bench wraps his leg in a plastic bag and, over the bag, puts on a tall leather boot.

"It's to help it slide on, otherwise it won't fit," he explains. "We always wear boots two sizes too small, so that they'll be tight and we have better control."

On the floor, in front of the mirror set into the wall, there's a wooden board. On the board, four members of a northern-style malambo quartet raise their chins to practice a look of arrogance and fierceness. Four chests rise, like four roosters preparing to fight. What happens next looks like a North Korean military parade: legs move in astonishing synchronization and eight heels step, scrape, stomp, strike, as if they were one. A circle of curious onlookers has formed around them to watch silently. When the men finish, a frozen ecstasy falls over them and the circle breaks up, as if they'd never been there, as if what they'd just seen was a sacred or secret ceremony, or both.

An hour later, at midnight, the doors to the five dressing rooms close, and from the other side of the flimsy metal doors we hear drums, guitars, total silence. Inside, readying their weapons, are the men that the crowd is waiting to see. Five competitors of the main malambo.

Every night the main malambo is announced in the same way. Between twelve thirty and one a.m. the Hymn of Laborde is played—"Dance the malambo/Argentina feels the life of its people/Laborde calls us to dance the national malambo"—and the announcer's voice says, "Ladies and gentlemen, the time has come for the category we've all been waiting for, here in Laborde and in the whole of Argentina!"

The announcer insists on including the whole of Argentina, every time, even though the whole of Argentina never hears him, and he continues, "Ladies and gentlemen, Laborde, the nation … it is now time for the main malambo category!"

Fireworks go off on the last lines of the song. When the announcer states the name of the hopeful who will dance, silence falls over the audience like a blanket of snow.

———————

The judges sit motionless at a long table below the stage.

The first sound is the strum of a guitar, sad like the last days of summer. The man who's going to dance wears a black corduroy jacket and a red vest. The fringe of the white *cribo* washes over his calves like a creamy rain, and in place of a *chiripá*, he wears dark skintight pants. He's blond, with a full beard. He walks to the center of the stage, stops, and with a movement that seems to spring from his bones, he caresses the floor with the toes of his boots, with his heel, with the side of his foot, a trail of precise blows, a succession of perfect sounds. Tense as a wolf ready to attack, the speed picks up little by little until his feet are two animals breaking, grinding, shattering, shredding, crushing, killing, and finally he pounds the stage with the force of a train crash and, bathed in sweat, stops, taut as a glass cord, his face tragic and purple. Then he bows reverently and leaves the stage. The voice of a woman, distant, indifferent, says:

"Time employed: four minutes, forty seconds."

That was the first main malambo I saw in the competition at Laborde, and it was like being attacked. I ran backstage and saw the man—Ariel Pérez, the hopeful from the province of Buenos Aires—rush into his dressing room with the urgency of someone repressing love or hate or the desire to kill.

"Awwww, look what you did to your tooooooe!"

Irma worriedly examines her son's toe, an enormous toe, sticking out of the horsehide boot, missing a strip of skin from the tip.

"Yeah, Ma, it's nothing."

"What do you mean nothing? You ripped off a piece. I'm going to look for a bandage and alcohol to disinfect it."

"Don't worry about it."

Irma doesn't listen and rushes to find alcohol, a bandage.

Pablo Albornoz sits looking at his toe as if he's seen it like that before. He's twenty-four years old, the hopeful from the Neuquén province who trained with Ariel Ávalos, and he's more worried about resting than about his toe. He has to dance again in an hour.

"Does it hurt?" I ask.

"Yes, but when you're up there you're so pumped that you can't feel it. It's four and a half minutes of grit and guts."

He works as the doorman at a day-care center, and he's already competed at Laborde many times, so many that he's begun to tell himself that maybe he's not cut out to win.

"I mean I must suck at this, I must be terrible. Because I've been dancing for twelve years and there are some guys who have danced only four years and they win the first time they compete. But I couldn't live if I didn't come."

Irma returns with a bottle of alcohol and a rag. She bends down and looks at the toe, which has left a bloody streak on the floor.

"Ay, you're missing a piece."

"Okay, Ma, we'll look at it later. I have to dance again now."

Irma disinfects the toe, Pablo puts on the plastic bag and the tall leather boot, and he begins his stretches. An injured toe, a plastic bag, and on top of that, a boot two sizes too small: it doesn't sound like anyone's idea of comfort.

"I always come with him," says Irma. "It's a sacrifice, because we got here Monday at eight a.m. by bus, a long, long trip, and his rehearsal time was for eleven a.m., so he got straight off the bus and came here. The next day he had his rehearsal at four in the morning, from four to seven. He makes such an effort. He has to pay his coach, pay for his flight, his stay, the classes.

And buy his outfits. But if they win, that changes everything, from a professional point of view, because they can make a living training others, having students, being judges. Pablo is still young, he's twenty-four, but if you don't win before you're thirty, forget it."

In Laborde the concept of former champion doesn't exist. Winning once means reigning forever, and the title implies, in addition to eternal prestige, an increase in work and improved pay. A dance instructor or a folklore specialist, as great as they may be, will never get $200 for a day of teaching or for judging a championship. While in front of the stage people dance, watch, applaud, eat, and take photos, backstage, enveloped in the smell of muscle cream, contestants await the moment when, perhaps, their lives will begin to change.

"People of Laborde, Argentina!" says the announcer enthusiastically. "These are the sons of our homeland, the ones who uphold the highest standards of our tradition! We'll be right back after a brief word from our sponsors."

———————

Hernán Villagra lives in a town called Los Altos, in Catamarca. He's twenty-four years old, studies criminology, hopes to join the police force—where his father works—and he lives in constant pain. Today, Friday, sitting at a table in the corner of the town square, he's in pain; when he stands and walks to the bathroom he's in pain. Pain is with him wherever he goes, because he has arthritis in his toes and surgery is the only solution. But first he has to complete the ritual: to dance the last solo malambo of his life on the stage at Laborde. Villagra was the 2010 champion, and he has spent the past year traveling, giving interviews, and signing autographs. At dawn on Monday morning he'll end his reign and hand over the title to the new champion, who will receive, from that moment on, the attention that had previously been his.

"I've been dancing since I was six years old. I competed here for the first time in 2007 and I was terrified. Not just anyone can get on that stage. The day we arrived my coach said to me 'Get changed, we're going to rehearse on the stage.' There were other hopefuls dancing the malambo, and I started to get scared. I got sick that day, I fainted, I was vomiting. But I danced and it turned out pretty good. I passed on to the finals, but I didn't win. In 2008, I was runner-up. And in 2009, I was runner-up again. To be runner-up two times is humiliating. I would have preferred to lose than to be runner-up again. It was horrible. To be so close and not make it. Also, you start to think how you have to work another whole year to compete again, and it wears you down physically. It's five minutes pounding on the boards. Your legs, your tendons, your cartilage all feel the effects; you wear yourself down, inside and out. The northern style gives you blisters and the southern burns your toes when you scrape the boards, you get splinters from the stage."

"And is it worth it to hurt yourself like that?" I ask.

"What you feel up there is like nothing else. It's like electricity. I competed again in 2010 and made it to the finals. And there I danced the best malambo of my life. When I got off the stage, I was blind. I was like in shock. And I won. On my way back to my town as the champion, my neighbors were waiting for me on the highway, and they made a caravan for the whole twelve miles into town."

"And now?"

"Now I don't want to think too much about my last malambo. I have to enjoy it, because it's the last. In that moment a lot of things probably go through your head."

"How do you think you're going to feel?"

"Well, a ton of emotions."

"Like what, for example?"

"Well, everything that's happened over the last year."

"Like what?"

"Everything I experienced."

I want to keep pressing. I begin to realize that it's useless.

"A ton of things go through your head." "So many emotions all at once." "It's something unforgettable." "You have to think like a champion." "Just representing my province here is a triumph." "People tell you amazing things."

The phrases sound like things that soccer players say to the press: "The team is very unified. Our spirits are very high. They had a better performance." When it comes time to answer concrete questions—how do they feel when they're dancing, what do they remember from the night they won the prize?—they repeat, one after another, the same set phrases: they mention the ton of emotions they felt or how wonderful everything was, but rarely can they recall concrete details. If I press them to tell me more, just one of all the wonderful things that happened to them, they'll tell the story of, for example, the 1996 champion who came up to give them a hug and told them, "What you do with the trophy is what gives it meaning," or the little boy who shook with emotion when they signed an autograph at a school in Patagonia. For them—sons of large families, raised in remote towns surrounded by rampant poverty and without a single famous relative—that's everything.

———————

"Look, this place is closed too. These Labordenses!"

Carlos de Santis, the representative from the province of Catamarca, drives around looking for a place to buy lunch. It's 12:36 p.m. but in Laborde everything closes at 12:30 and doesn't open back up until four or five in the afternoon. Not even the two thousand people who come for the week of the festival alter the regular schedule of lunch break and siesta. To Carlos de Santis, dance instructor and coach to the two other malambo champions from Catamarca—Diego Argañaraz, who won in 2006, and Hernán Villagra—this seems perfectly normal: he's from a town of one thousand inhabitants called Graneros, in the province of Tucumán.

"I lived in a little house with mud walls and a thatched roof. The refrigerator was just a hole we dug in the floor and covered with a wet cloth, and that's where we put things so that they'd stay cool. I would go into the woods and cut firewood to sell. Or I'd go hunt frogs and sell them. Since I wanted to study, I would leave my house at five in the morning and walk three hours to school. It started at eight and let out at twelve and I'd get back home at four. At five in the afternoon, I'd go out to work in the fields until the sun went down. At night I would go to a little bar to wait on tables and sweep up, they'd pay me with a *milanesa* for dinner and the tips. One day some-one came to town to teach malambo, and I went. I wanted to learn everything: malambo, English, piano— whatever I could to get me out of that town. Not because I didn't like it there, but I didn't want to end up working in the fields, in the woods. I think that's why the malambo means so much to us. We're humble people who understand suffering. Like the malambo. And we have to tell the boys to show that, that essence. To de-fend the tradition. But it's a huge sacrifice, because you have to train for 365 days to dance for five minutes. And if they make a mistake in those five minutes, good-bye to a year of work. And they're very humble kids, everything costs them a lot."

At one p.m., when it's clear that nothing in town is open, Carlos de Santis stops the car in front of the Mariano Moreno School, where his team is staying.

"Come in. You can meet everyone."

On the playground, under a dense heat, clothes hang on a line and a few men sit playing cards. Inside, the school looks like a refugee camp. In the warm breeze created by five fans, the floor is covered with mattresses, which in turn are covered in blankets, towels, hats, dresses, guitars, drums, people. On the walls, someone has hung signs that read PLEASE HELP KEEP THE SPACE CLEAN AND ORDERLY FOR THE COM-FORT OF EVERYONE. Here and there are thermoses, maté gourds, maté, sugar, baby bottles, boxes of off-brand juice, *dulce de leche*, tea bags, bread, diapers, cookies. The windows are draped with ponchos, and a few women are ironing the dresses they'll wear that night. The heat is so thick that it's almost a fog. Carlos de Santis points to a corner of one of the classrooms and says:

"That's where I sleep."

In the corner, there's simply a mattress.

———————

Their average age is twenty-three. They don't smoke, they don't drink, they don't stay up late. Many of them listen to punk or heavy metal or rock, but all are able to differentiate a *pericón* from a Chilean *cueca*, a waltz from a *vidala*. They have pored over books such as *Martín Fierro, Don Segundo Sombra,* and *Juan Moreira*: epitomes of the gaucho tradition. These sagas and certain period movies—like *The Gaucho War*—are as inspiring for them as *Harry Potter* or *Star Trek* is for others. They place importance on words such as *respect, tradition, nation, flag*. They want to have, onstage but also offstage, the attributes commonly ascribed to gauchos—austerity, courage, pride, sincerity, directness—and to be rugged and strong enough to endure the blows they've always taken. That they still take.

———————

Héctor Aricó is a dancer, choreographer, researcher, author of books and articles on traditional Argentinian dances. He's been a judge at Laborde for fifteen years and he has an impeccable reputation. Today, Friday, he's been at the judges' table, like every day, from eight at night to six in the morning. He gave a talk on attire at ten this morning. He now stands smoking under an awning in the field, dressed in black, carefully modulating his words and gesticulating a lot, as if he were an actor in a silent film.

"Laborde doesn't have the recognition that other festivals have at the commercial level, because the organizing committee and the delegates have preferred it that way. But it's the bastion of the malambo, and for a dancer it's the highest recognition."

"What things are the judges evaluating when they watch the dancers?"

"First of all, symmetry. This is a perfectly symmetrical dance by a human figure that's naturally asymmetrical. The first step in training—and the biggest challenge—is to create symmetry: in ability, intensity, sound, in spatial equality. The second problem is stamina. Here, everyone knows they're not going to win with a two- or three-minute malambo: they have to get close to five. So the capacity for stamina is also evaluated. Then the structure, which has to be attractive, but also has to be within the regulations: we have to see, for example, that the legs aren't raised above the limits, because this isn't a show, it's a competition. And the musical accompaniment—often the musicians don't really accompany the malambo dancer, and instead the music becomes the protagonist and detracts from the dance. And last, the attire: the design on their ponchos must correspond to the correct province, and the *bombachas* can't have too many pleats. For these boys, when they win, an important labor market opens up for them, but it's also a premature retirement. They become champions at twenty-one, twenty-two years old, and it's a dance they'll never do again. There's no regulation prohibiting it, but what's at stake is the idea, 'And if I sign up for that festival and they beat me? It's better to keep my glory.'"

"Just one, on the stage: that's what I need from you guys."

Early afternoon, under a brutal sun, a malambo quartet rehearses onstage. They wear brightly colored shirts, surfer shorts, and their feet are bare. The coach repeats:

"I don't need anything else. Together, together, together. Just one." They stomp on the floor as if they're trying to get a confession out of it. Meanwhile, sitting under the shade of the eucalyptus trees, Pablo Sánchez, the delegate from Tucumán, speaks to a group of girls and boys who look at him with worried faces.

"We have to be strong. Other festivals are fine, but Laborde is in a higher category. It's the heavyweight category. This is the first time it's happened in fifty-five years of dance, and we'll figure out where to get the money to pay for the bus. You guys don't need to worry about that, only about putting everything into your performance on the stage."

The crowd nods and disperses. Sánchez—patriarch of a family of malambo dancers from Tucumán, who's trained six champions and two runners-up—explains that the bus that was supposed to bring them from Tucumán, and which they'd already paid for, never showed up. They had to hire another bus at the last minute and, of course, pay for the trip a second time.

"We got ourselves into a lot of debt, but we'll find a way to work it out."

"You didn't consider canceling the trip?"

"Never. Not coming to Laborde is unthinkable."

Pablo Sánchez's oldest son, Damián, was destined to become the next grand champion at Laborde when, at twenty years old, he was killed by a brain aneurism. So his younger brother, Marcelo, entered the competition and took the title in 1995.

"The power of the dance is in the soul, in the heart. Outside is all technique. Your tapping has to be perfect, you have to know how to stand, stick the instep, increase your energy, your attitude. But the malambo requires a much stronger expression than other dances, so apart from just knowing the technique, you have to be able to feel the boards, understand them, bang yourself into the stage. The day you lose that, you lose everything. You have to feel it blow by blow. Like the beat of a heart. The message has to clearly reach the people."

"What message is that?"

"The message is: Here I am. I come from this land."

"I named him Fausto after *Fausto*. I think *criollos* have to remain *criollos* in everything. I don't like names like Brian or Jonathan. And besides, with my last name, Cortez, it doesn't go."

Fausto, by the nineteenth-century Argentinian writer Estanislao del Campo, is an emblematic work of gaucho literature, and it's also the name Víctor Cortez gave his son. Cortez is the 1987 champion from Córdoba and persona non grata according to the festival's organizing committee due to a labor lawsuit he filed against them after losing his job as an instructor at a dance school in town.

"The champions have some privileges. They don't pay the entrance fee, they eat for free. I have to pay for my ticket to get in, I have to pay to eat, but the worst thing is that I can't accompany my hopefuls backstage. It's like having a kid you've taken care of all year, and then he has his mother taken away at the last minute. This is the most important moment—when you're putting on your boots, when you're getting dressed like a gaucho, when you feel the malambo growing inside you."

Today Víctor Cortez works as a welder at a company that manufactures buses, and he says that, from time to time, his coworkers find an article about him and they're shocked. "And they say: 'Look who this old man who works with us is.'"

He's seated on a bench in the town square. The bars around it begin to fill up, and on the grass, groups of young men and women play the guitar or dance. This year, Cortez trained Rodrigo Heredia, from Córdoba, who will compete for the first time in the main malambo category.

"He's a beautiful kid. Healthy, clean. You can make them into artists, but not into good people. When I came to Laborde, I thought I was the best of them all. They could have put God in front of me and I'd have said: 'I'm better than God.' And well, you have to work with them on that in some way. So that they don't lose their humility, but up there they can still say: 'I'm the best.'"

"And if they lose?" I ask.

"It's painful. But life doesn't end here."

———————

Exhaustion sets in after two minutes. Someone with an average level of training could dance, without too much effort, a malambo that lasts that long. But after two minutes, the body keeps going only thanks to the intense training and the flood of endorphins that try to block out the panic of suffocation, the contraction of muscles, the pain in the joints, the expectant gazes of six thousand people, and the scrutiny of a jury that registers every last breath. Maybe that's why when they get off the stage they all seem like they've just gone through some unspeakable experience, some traumatic event.

———————

Although during the day the temperature can exceed 104 degrees Fahrenheit, at night, without fail, it drops dramatically. Today, Friday the fourteenth, twelve thirty a.m., it must be around 55 degrees, but backstage it looks like Carnival. There are bodies dressing and undressing, sweat, music, rushing. Darío Flores, the hopeful for the province of La Rioja, leaves the stage as they all do: blind from the exertion, crucified, his gaze absent and his hands on his hips, fighting to catch his breath. Someone hugs him, and like a person coming out of a trance he says, "Thank you. Thank you." I watch and think I recognize a pattern: the same exasperating tension when they're in the dressing rooms, the same blazing explosion as they perform, the same agony and the exact same ecstasy after they've finished. Then I hear, from onstage, the strum of a guitar. There's something in that strum—something like the tension of an animal crouching low to the ground, ready to pounce—that captures my attention. So I turn around and run, ducking down, to find a seat behind the judges' table.

It's the first time I see Rodolfo González Alcántara.

And what I see leaves me speechless.

Why did he stand out? He looked just like anyone else. He wore a beige jacket, gray vest, bowler hat, red *chiripá*, and a black tie. Why did he stand out for me when I couldn't even tell the difference between a really great dancer and a mediocre one? But there he was—Rodolfo González Alcántara, twenty-eight years old, the hopeful from La Pampa, gigantic—and there I was, sitting on the grass, speechless. When he finished dancing, the distant, indifferent voice of the female announcer declared, "Time employed: four minutes fifty-two seconds."

And that was the exact moment when this story turned into something else. A difficult story. The story of an ordinary man.

That Friday night, Rodolfo González Alcántara moved to the center of the stage like a hurricane-force gale, like a puma, like a stag, like a robber of souls, and he remained nailed to the spot for two or three beats, his brow furrowed, staring at something that no one else could see. The first movement of his legs made his *cribo* tremble like a soft sea creature rocked by the waves. Then, for four minutes and fifty-two seconds, he made the night crackle with his blows.

It was the open field, it was the dusty ground, it was the taut horizon of the pampa, it was the smell of horses, the sound of the summer sky, the buzz of solitude, it was fury, sickness, war, it was the antithesis of peace. It was the blade and the cut. It was all devouring. It was punishment. When he was finished, he pounded the stage with a monstrous force, froze on the spot, and stood staring out through the fine layers of the night, covered in stars, all ablaze. And, half-smiling—like a prince, like a ruffian, or like the devil—he tipped his hat. And he left the stage.

That's how it was.

I don't know if they applauded him. I don't remember.

What did I do after that? I remember because I took these notes. I ran backstage and tried to find him in the tumult—a huge man, dressed in a hat and a red poncho tied at the waist, someone who wouldn't be hard to spot—but I didn't see him anywhere. Until finally, in front of the open door to one of the dressing rooms, I saw a very short man, no more than five feet tall, without jacket or vest or bowler hat. I recognized him because he was panting. He was alone. I went up to him. I asked him where he was from.

"From Santa Rosa, La Pampa," he told me, with that voice I would hear so many times afterward and that peculiar manner of snuffing out the end of his sentences like someone who assigns himself little importance. "But I live in Buenos Aires. I'm a dance instructor."

He shook, his hands and legs shook, his fingers shook as he stroked the beard that barely covered his chin, and I asked him his name.

"Rodolfo. Rodolfo González Alcántara."

In that moment, according to my notes, the announcer said something that sounded like "Marín Mills, the flour that fights high cholesterol." I didn't write anything else that night. It was two o'clock in the morning.

It's Saturday and I'm following behind Fernando Castro and Sebastián Sayago. Fernando Castro is Rodolfo González Alcántara's coach and also accompanies him on guitar. He won the title of champion in 2009, at twenty-one years old, and his brother Sebastián Sayago, three years older, is the hopeful from the province of Santiago del Estero, the state that has produced the most champions. There's a strange connection between these three men. Sebastián Sayago is the brother of

Fernando Castro, who is coach and guitar player for Rodolfo, who is Sebastián Sayago's competition. And although they've known each other forever, Fernando Castro didn't find out that Sebastián Sayago was his brother until the age of nineteen.

Sebastián Sayago is tall and skinny. His skin, eyes, hair, and beard are all very dark, and he sits in the patio of the house he's rented along with seven other people. He lives in Santiago, the capital of his province, with his mother and ten-year-old sister Milena. He's been dancing since he was four. He's now twenty-six, and for the past five years he's been traveling the world performing malambo shows on luxury cruise ships. In Laborde, he sleeps next to one of his teammates, in the same bed, because there aren't enough beds for everyone.

He says, "People ask me: 'But why are you going to go dance in Laborde, when you can make money traveling the world?' But they don't understand what this means to me. The stage at Laborde is like no other. To stand on those boards where so many other souls have stood, so many champions. Before I go on, I ask those souls for permission to dance."

This is the third time he's entered in the main malambo category—he competed in 2006 and 2010—but he's never made it to the finals.

"I canceled a lot of contracts with cruise ships so that I could stay in Santiago and train. It's a sacrifice, because I have to help my mom and my little sister, who's like a daughter to me, she's the light of my life, but I had to do this. I get up at six, go running, I practice my steps. And you have to train your attitude, your posture, your aggressive stare, show your gaucho face. You spend hours looking at yourself in the mirror, trying to find your fiercest look. I try to look like I'm coming to claim my territory, to defend something. And when I go onstage I try to feel like I'm lit up. Like with every move I want to give people goose bumps. You generally start with a slow rhythm, and then you make things more difficult and speed up the rhythm to show your skill, precision, strength, and you end with endurance. When you get going really fast you turn your soul over to the malambo, because your muscles are so tired at that point and the dance is your life and soul—you give it everything you have."

Sebastián has thin dark feet and he's barefoot, because when he danced the northern style he got blisters that burst when he danced the southern style.

"I covered the stage in blood, but when you're on the boards you don't feel pain. You become a giant. You're a gigantic person and there's nothing else around you."

His father left when his mother was pregnant with him, and Sebastián first met him when he was ten years old. The man already had another family with three children, of which Fernando Castro is the oldest.

"Fernando and I met on the folklore scene in Santiago, because both of us ended up dancing. I knew he was my brother, everyone knew. He was the only one who didn't know. And one day someone said to him: 'Tell your brother I said hello.' And he said, 'Which brother?' 'Sebastián.' And he came and asked me."

"And what did you say to him?"

"I put my hand on his shoulder and I said: 'Yes, Fer, sit down, let's talk.'"

"How did he take it?"

"Good, very good. Fer and I are good friends."

The year he won, Fernando Castro beat out Sebastián Sayago in the first qualifying round, meaning that in 2009, although he'd trained hard, Sayago wasn't able to participate in the festival.

"I was on a boat, in Australia, when I found out that Fer had been named champion. I was in my cabin, with a fourteen-hour time difference, watching everything on the computer, and I was sitting there all alone just crying."

"Did you feel jealous?"

"Nooo. I felt happy. Proud. Sad that I couldn't be there. If someone from Santiago wins, for me it's the best. And if it's my brother, better yet."

"And what are you going to do with the trophy if you win?"

"I'm going to give it to my grandfather."

———————

Fernando Castro is in the pressroom, wearing jeans and a red shirt with what looks like a rosary peeking out. His long hair is pulled back in a bun, still wet from a recent bath.

"You have to take care of your image. I was champion in 2009, so I have to be well-dressed and not set a bad example. They're always going to be looking at you harder because you're a champion."

He's been dancing since he was ten years old and now lives in San Fernando, about forty kilometers outside Buenos Aires, where he studies folklore, but he finds it hard to keep up with city life.

"Going into the city every day on the train is hard for me. I'm always late. I miss Santiago. I had my birdcages there, I took a siesta every day. In Buenos Aires everything is rushed. I don't like it. In Santiago I went fishing, I caught birds. I'm very patient and I can spend hours fishing."

"What do you think about while you're fishing?"

"About nothing. I watch the water flow by."

No one knew Fernando Castro when, at twenty-one, he competed for the first time in the main malambo category at Laborde. Since he looks five or six years younger than he is, and he's very short, everyone asked him if he was there to compete in the special youth category, for dancers under twenty. But his dance had the effect of a meteorite hitting the earth. Northern is his strong style, and he gave his all in a brave and brilliant dance with tapping and stomping that astonished everyone and snatched the championship from Hernán Villagra, the previous year's runner-up and therefore the favorite for that year.

"When I entered the competition I had to overcome this baby face. I was new; no one would have bet a cent on me, I was small. But I was well-trained."

"Who trained you?"

"I trained myself, on my own. I invented a method. I went out running and I thought about the malambo. I ran with attitude. I walked with attitude. I showered with attitude. To get into character I watched gaucho movies, *Juan Moreira, Martín*

Fierro, to see what the gaucho was like, how he suffered, how he walked. Because I wanted to transmit the idea of a man, a gaucho, with this baby face and no beard. I was just finally able to grow this beard, which is barely three hairs. But when I danced, the people stood up and started applauding, and I went offstage very happy. And then they said that I was the champion. And the interviews started, television and radio, and I was quiet, shy. No one had ever taught me to talk. I had to learn. And the next year, the day I had to turn over the title, all my emotions hit me at once."

"What did you feel?"

"That something was ending. I can't dance anymore. Because they won't let me here. If not, I would compete in other places. But it's like a pact to defend the title. If you lose somewhere else, it's like you bring the festival down with you. But I like the idea that my students can be my eyes, my soul, my feet up onstage."

"Does it bother you that the festival is so little-known?"

"No, no. There aren't many festivals like this one that maintain their tradition, that aren't gimmicky, that aren't just trying to get applause, that don't have electric guitar."

Fernando Castro was a skateboarder, he practiced judo and karate. In addition to folkloric music, he listened to and still listens to punk (he likes an Argentinian group, Flema) and rock (he likes El Otro Yo, Dos Minutos, Andrés Calamaro), and he says that his friends always understood that these tastes were compatible with total sobriety.

"Just in the last two years I've started to try a little alcohol. But I've never gotten drunk. I represent my province, and I can't make it look bad."

His parents never saw him dance at Laborde because they couldn't afford the trip, so the year he was named champion Fernando came to town with his uncle, Enrique Castro, who had just had surgery to remove a tumor.

"He gave me faith, he told me to read the Bible, to pray. He doesn't know anything about malambo. He saw me dance for the first time here, but he was really impressed. I get onstage and I feel like King Kong—everyone's tiny and I'm huge. And I try to find that inner calm, so that inside everything is slow and outside I'm faster than anyone. For me, malambo is like a story. My malambo has twenty-three figures and every figure has a feeling. The first one is like your calling card. You show that you're skilled, that you have intensity, ability, presence. And then it's like you start to tell your story: this is what I've suffered and this is what I've experienced."

"Have you been through a lot?"

"I'm from a very humble family. I've done everything to get a little money. In my family the only one who works is my dad, he drives a bus in Santiago, and there are three of us kids. Well, four. I have a brother, Sebastián Sayago, who's my dad's son. We met on the scene, because we both dance, but I didn't know he was my brother, and one day an instructor told me: 'Say hello to your brother for me.' And I asked him: 'Which brother?' And he tells me: 'Sebas.' And I went and asked him and it turned out he already knew. I was so proud to have an older brother who did the same thing I did. That both of us could represent the province, my country."

"You weren't mad at your father?"

"No, no, I really wasn't. I wondered why he wouldn't have told me. But I didn't bring it up with my dad. I never told him that I knew, but he figured it out later on his own. My younger siblings don't know that Sebas is my brother. But I don't know if it's my responsibility to tell them. I don't think so. I think the right thing would be for my dad to tell them, right?"

Saturday night, the hopeful from Mendoza is in dressing room 5 with the walls that don't reach the ceiling. The door is closed, but the strum of the guitar bursts through like a tangible object, a wall of adrenaline and forewarning. When it's his turn to go on, the hopeful walks to the stage with his brow creased, not looking at anyone. And what I see in his face is what I see, every night, on all of their faces: certainty of the most absolute solitude, relief and fear in knowing that, finally, their time has come.

A hopeful in the main malambo category, getting ready to dance the northern malambo, looks like a bull about to charge. That night, at four in the morning, a man gets onstage like he's declaring war on the universe. He plants himself in the center of the stage and waits a few seconds, his legs apart, the wings of his scarf brushing against his chest with deceptive innocence. The first figures are almost serene—made with boots that, like everyone's, have nails in the heels to make them sound louder. The legs of his *bombachas* ruffle slightly, like two slow jellyfish, and the man, with his chin raised, bends his ankles, scrapes his soles, stands on his heels, and thrashes. His upright torso follows the movements easily, as if his body were a marble column covered in flesh. After a minute and a half, every time he turns, a small crown of sweat forms around his head. At three minutes, the malambo is a wall of sound, a jumble of boots, drum, and guitar that picks up speed at an asphyxiating rate. At four minutes, his feet pound the stage with savage fury, the guitar, drum, and boots are a solid mass of blows, and at four minutes fifty seconds, the man lowers his head, raises one leg, and with colossal force, bashes it into the wood, his heart monstrously swollen, with the lucid yet frenzied expression of someone who's just experienced a revelation. After a few seconds of unnatural stillness, in which the public claps and shouts, the man, like someone emptying a gun into a dead body, dances off the stage with a short and furious storm of tapping, and every cell in his body seems to scream: *This is what I'm made of. I am capable of absolutely anything.*

It's Sunday, eleven in the morning. Today the judges announce the names of the dancers who will move on to the finals, and Laborde breathes with a combination of anxiety and resignation.

Hugo "Cheeks" Moreyra, the 2004 champion from Santa

Fe, is in the field, sitting under the awning that covers the grill area, shielding himself from a light rain. He's thirty-one years old and he says that now, like all champions, he's fat.

"When you stop training, you gain weight immediately. You can spot us former champions by our bellies. It takes too much willpower to say: 'I made it to Laborde, I won the championship, and I'm going to keep training three more years.'"

Moreyra is not fat, but if you compare his current body to that of the rail-thin man who won the championship seven years earlier, you can tell some things have changed, the most noteworthy being the size of his belly which, in 2004, was nonexistent.

"When I won, I felt like a weight had been lifted off me. I competed as a hopeful for four years. I had been runner-up in 2003, and I said 'If I don't win, I'm not competing anymore.' Training was getting really hard on me."

He's the son of a homemaker and a metalworker, and he started dancing at the age of four in a local ballet company where he took the place of his sister, who was sick but didn't want to lose her spot. He won the championship at Laborde after just five months of training, because a muscle strain and a sprained ankle had him in and out of casts and physical therapy between April and August.

"But no one knows that that happened to me, I didn't tell anyone. If you tell people, they start to bring you down: 'Oh, poor thing, how are you ever going to dance, it's going to be even harder for you.' And you give them an advantage: it's not the same to compete against someone who's just getting over an injury as with someone who was training all year long.

But I won. Of course winning at Laborde is like cutting your legs off. You can keep competing in other categories, in team malambo, in dance duos, but not as a soloist. We come to win knowing that we're going to lose. And on top of that, only the people who come to Laborde know about it, outside no one knows what it is."

"Do you wish more people knew about it?"

"No, not at all. Those of us who are involved in the dance know that this is the greatest honor, and that's enough. You could be an expert in folklore, a PhD in whatever, but if you're a champion at Laborde, that comes first."

Moreyra's cell phone rings and he answers it. When he hangs up he says, "They have the names."

Competing in the finals are the 2010 runner-up (Gonzalo "Pony" Molina), the hopeful from Tucumán, the hopeful from Buenos Aires, and Rodolfo González Alcántara, who, like the runner-up, represents the province of La Pampa.

Rodrigo Heredia is twenty-three years old. He has a beard, and his hair is pulled back tightly at the nape of his neck. He's staying with members of several teams in a building that was once a retirement home. Unlike almost everyone else, he hasn't gone out to the *peña*, the place where, once the festival has finished for the day, the dancing continues until eleven in the morning. He does not drink alcohol; he does not stay up late. During his time in Laborde he maintains the same monastic lifestyle he leads the rest of the year.

"You have to take good care of yourself. The smallest thing you do, they'll find out and you look bad."

The hopefuls for the main malambo category—and the champions of previous years—stick to a code of conduct based on the old axiom that it's not only important to be a certain way but also to appear that way to others. Therefore, for any hopeful—or previous champion—rumors related to alcohol, partying, or even sloppy dress and hygiene can permanently damage their reputation.

Now it's mid-afternoon on Sunday. Dressed in jeans and a yellow shirt, standing in the dark hallway of the retirement home, Rodrigo Heredia says that the advantage of staying there is that it's quieter than other places and the rooms have private bathrooms. There's no bathroom in his room, but he has a mattress, a closet, a bag with his clothes already packed, and the gaucho outfit, which for the rest of this year won't be worn again. Earlier that day, when his coach Víctor Cortez found out that Rodrigo would not be going on to the finals, he found him and said, "Son, I'm grateful for everything you've done for me. The bad news is that we're not in the finals." Rodrigo responded, "Well, coach, I only want to be what you were hoping for."

"Now I have to start saving money for next year," says Rodrigo.

———

Marcos Pratto lives in Unquillo, where he runs a production company, but he was born and raised in Laborde, and he's the only local champion.

"I trained with Víctor Cortez. I first competed in 2002 and I was a finalist. And the next year I won. I was the only hopeful ever from Laborde. There has never been another. But when I started dancing, at twelve, my classmates laughed at me, they thought it was for old people. Today you see kids walking around town carrying a guitar. They dance on the street corners, but it wasn't like that before."

He's thirty-two, of average height, and has a serious expression as he sits in the pressroom. Now, aside from working in the production company, he trains other hopefuls, but he says he won't compete again in any category because he feels fat and he wants people to remember him as he was the year he won.

"But not being able to drink alcohol or smoke, taking care of yourself and working out, I don't think it has to be seen as a sacrifice. It's just what you have to do if you want to achieve something. That's why making people from the main category dance at four in the morning is disrespectful. All year long, you're telling the kid that he has to practice, not stay up late, eat healthy, and the day he has to compete in the most important competition of his life, you put him through hell all night. The dressing rooms are horrible, you're warming up to go onstage and you have two hundred people walking by you, there's one bathroom for three hundred people. And the committee wants to see the former champions at the festival every year, but they don't give us anything. We have to pay for the trip, accommodation. But on the other hand I come here, I hear the hymn, and I get goose bumps. It moves me to see the kids, see the dreams they have. It's our seven, eight days of glory. And then, ciao, you go back to being anonymous."

"And could you go a few years without coming?"

"No way. I'd die."

On Sunday night, an hour before he's set to go onstage to dance in the finals, Rodolfo González Alcántara and his coach, Fernando Castro, are getting dressed in the loft above the pressroom because there aren't enough dressing rooms. Rodolfo takes his clothes out of his brown bag and puts on his horsehide boots, which he tightens first with the leather straps, then with tape, and he slicks down his hair with water. His toes are white with calluses, his toenails thick as wood. When he's halfway dressed—without vest, jacket, or hat—he goes down, and in front of the mirror that covers the walls of the room, he rehearses a few figures of his malambo. His gaze is distant, as if he were trying to protect himself from a fire burning inside. When he finishes, he says, "Ready to go?"

"Ready," I say.

A main malambo quartet has just danced, and in the dressing rooms, there are euphoric embraces, the signs of a performance that went well. Someone points Rodolfo to a dressing room and he opens the door. Inside, sleeping, is Hernán Villagra, who wakes up to greet him.

"Hello."

"Hello."

Then he stands up and leaves. Fernando Castro sets his guitar down and examines the folds of Rodolfo's *chiripá*.

"It's long on this side and short on this one. Take it off."

Rodolfo takes off the *chiripá*, and Fernando Castro, with an imperturbable patience, as if he were dressing a child or a bullfighter, straightens his folds, tightens his sash, his tie. Finally, he asks:

"All right?"

Rodolfo nods, mute.

"Come on, enjoy it, we're in the finals," says Fernando, and since he has to go onstage a little earlier, like all the musicians who accompany the dancers, he heads there now, leaving us alone.

Rodolfo begins to pace back and forth like a caged and rabid tiger. He opens his backpack, takes out a book with a blue cover, sets it on the cement counter, and without ceasing his movement, begins to read. The book is a copy of the Bible, and Rodolfo whispers with his head bent over the pages. He looks at once submissive and invincible and tremendously fragile. His neck is tilted at an angle that says, without saying it, "I'm in your hands," and his fingers are interlocked in a gesture of prayer. And as I stare at the back of this man whom I know nothing about, who reads the words of his God before he goes out to gamble it all, an uncomfortable certainty flares up inside me: this is the most frighteningly intimate situation that I've ever shared with another human being. Something in him desperately screams, "Don't look at me!" But I'm there to look. And I look.

After a few minutes, Rodolfo closes the book, kisses it, and returns it to his backpack. He picks up his cell phone, and the song "Be You," by Almafuerte, an Argentinian rock band, begins to play: "Let's go, man, don't let/your dreams go to waste./If you're not you, it would be sad./If you're not you, it would be very sad." It's two thirty in the morning when, finally, Rodolfo dances.

———————

He descends the stage soaked, and he quickly enters the dressing room. He takes off his jacket and sits with his arms hanging between his legs. Fernando Castro enters, followed by a small dark-skinned woman with long shiny hair and almond-shaped eyes. It's Miriam Carrizo, a dancer and Rodolfo's girlfriend of nine years. They hug, they talk about things that I don't understand related to rhythm and the figures. Then Rodolfo waits. And Fernando Castro waits. And Miriam Carrizo waits. And I wait.

At six thirty in the morning, the day already bright, Hernán Villagra dances his last malambo, he says good-bye, he cries, and the announcer declares, with much fanfare, the results: Gonzalo "Pony" Molina, from the province of La Pampa, is the champion. And the runner-up, from the same province, is Rodolfo González Alcántara.

Two months go by before I see him again in Buenos Aires.

———————

I think the first thing that throws me off is his clothing. Throughout the four days I spent in Laborde I only saw Rodolfo González Alcántara dressed as a gaucho. This morning in late March, at a café in Buenos Aires, he shows up in jeans— the cuffs rolled up—a black jacket, and a backpack over one shoulder.

"Hello, how are you?" he says.

Rodolfo is twenty-eight years old, his hair is dark and wavy, not very long, his beard is sparse. A goatee barely covers his chin and moves in a thin line up to his lower lip, giving him the look of a swashbuckler or a pirate. His jaw is square, his brown eyes sparkle constantly with laughter and, when he dances, cast an inexplicable, almost suicidal magnetism over his entire face. It's eleven a.m. and he's just left the hospital where he'd been to visit his nephew. The café is small with old Formica tables, in a neighborhood near the city center, a few blocks from the IUNA, the National University Art Institute, where Rodolfo studied folklore and where he's now the head instructor of Technique in Performance Tap. I ask him—although I already know the answer—if what he was reading that night in Laborde, as he waited to go onstage, was the Bible, and he says it was. He opens his black backpack, takes out the same blue-covered book, and tells me that he carries it with him always.

"I open it and I read at any point and sometimes it's incredible, because what I read relates exactly to that moment in my life."

Now his days are spent between teaching classes in the IUNA and a few public schools and his training sessions with Fernando Castro.

"Were you happy to be named runner-up?" I ask.

"Yes. But Fernando and I were going over everything and there were a lot of things that I missed."

"What things?"

"My vest started riding up during the finals, because I had accidentally hooked it onto my jacket. I realized it when I was about to go on, and I thought, Oh well, too late. I was confident in the malambo. I went on and I thought, This is mine. But I got distracted, I didn't give it my all. Freddy Vacca, who was the champion for 1996, told me: 'You have to go onstage and leave everything there, till there's nothing left. You empty yourself out, and the audience takes it all.'"

The audience takes it all. Is that what happened to me?

***

Rodolfo González Alcántara is the son of María Luisa Alcántara and a man whose name he will never utter because, for him, his only father is Rubén Carabajal, his mother's second husband. Rodolfo's full name was Luis Rodolfo Antonio González until, when he turned sixteen, he went to the Santa Rosa city hall and said "I want to change my last name from González." Since that wasn't possible, he added his mother's last name, Alcántara, and now his name is Luis Rodolfo Antonio González Alcántara. He has two younger siblings and four older ones with whom he has only sporadic contact. His mother and biological father were married when they were fourteen and sixteen years old: his father was the son of radical evangelicals who believed that a man should marry his first girlfriend, and he obeyed. The children came soon after. One, two, four. By the time María Luisa became pregnant with the fifth, she had long been receiving beatings, the scars from which still remain, but she never expected her husband to say, "And what are you planning to do with this baby that's not even mine?" So, pregnant, she left with her four young children and the fifth on the way. Rodolfo came into the world on February 13, 1983. Shortly thereafter, his paternal grandfather took his older siblings—saying it was just for a visit—and never returned. Rubén Carabajal was a welder; he was eighteen when he met Rodolfo's mother through her brothers. As soon as he heard that the woman he'd always admired had become single, he approached her. He had no reservations about starting a relationship with a woman who had a baby—and four other children—but shortly thereafter he was called to complete his obligatory military service. Rodolfo hadn't even learned to talk when he began to suffer repeated bouts of pneumonia that landed him, again and again, in the hospital with fevers and convulsions. To make the baby's stays easier, Rubén Carabajal found the perfect excuse: he would go to the hospital to donate blood. On the days when he donated blood, he was allowed to stay a bit longer with María Luisa and the baby, who regularly suffered crises that led the nuns to sprinkle him with holy water, a process believed to keep dying babies from being trapped in limbo, between heaven and hell. But the baby survived, Rubén Carabajal finished his military service and returned to his job as a welder, and they all moved into a ten-by-ten-foot room with a leaky tin roof. The bathroom was outside, near the well they used to get water. Two more children soon arrived: Diego and a girl they called Chiri. At twenty-seven, María Luisa was diagnosed with arthritis in her joints and had to quit working. The family suffered through long periods in which there was not enough to eat, living on tortillas made from flour and water.

———————

At eight years old, Rodolfo González was very short, very fat, and he wanted to dance. No one in his family had ever danced before but he began taking malambo lessons with a man named Daniel Echaide after school. Rodolfo was an outstanding student despite the fact that his parents couldn't afford books or even the most basic materials. When there wasn't money to buy the items needed for arts-and-crafts projects, Rodolfo gathered sticks, sharpened them to a neat point, and used them in art class to carve his name, or the logo of his soccer team, into pieces of wood. He studied malambo with Daniel Echaide for two years, then joined a group called El Salitral, and at age eleven joined Mamüll Mapú, a folkloric dance company, for four years, traveling with the group to festivals in Olavarría, Santa Fe, and Córdoba, and winning top prizes. At twelve, he competed for the first time in Laborde, in the junior malambo category, and he experienced something that had never happened before: he came in second and discovered that, for him, that was the same as not even competing. In 1996 he trained after school with the Mamüll group and in the mornings with Sergio Pérez, that year's champion from the province of La Pampa, who had offered to train him free of charge. In 1997, he entered again in the same category and won. In 2000 he was the youth champion, and in 2003 the runner-up in the special youth category.

Meanwhile, his parents built a house thanks to a government program called Individual Effort: the state provides the land and the materials and the beneficiaries build the house with their own hands. When Rodolfo finished high school—still a star student—he thought that he'd like to work as a prison guard in order to make a decent salary. He had worked a bit with Rubén in construction and sometimes stole corn which he then sold, but he needed a steady job. He found out the requirements for the entrance exam and started studying to be a prison guard. But one day a teacher asked him, "Are you sure that's what you want to do? You're different, I can see you as a teacher, but not in a prison. And what you aren't able to do when you're young you'll pass down to your children: failure, frustration." Rodolfo reconsidered. Before even obtaining the test results—although he was declared ineligible due to misdiagnosis of a neurological issue—he knew that he didn't really want to go down that career path. Instead, in 2001, he began giving music lessons at a school in the nearby town of Guatraché. Soon afterward the school told him that someone from the IUNA would be coming by to supervise him. The thought of someone judging whether his work was good or bad bothered Rodolfo, and so he decided to move to Buenos Aires to study.

After our first meeting in the café, I walked with him back to the IUNA. By the time we said our good-byes, it was clear to me that Rodolfo's story was that of a man who had awakened the most dangerous of emotions: hope.

An ordinary man raised by ordinary parents who fought to have a better life in ordinary poverty is no more extraordinary than many from poor families. Are we interested in reading stories about people like Rodolfo? People who believe that family is important, that goodness and God exist? Are we interested in poverty when it's not extreme, when it doesn't involve violence, when it's free from the brutality that we love to see it—read it—dressed in?

At age five, he asked why his last name was González when his siblings' last name was Carabajal. Rubén and María Luisa explained that his father lived with his four older siblings, far away. Rodolfo has always had a distant relationship with the man. He'd recently traveled to General Pico, a city in La Pampa, to visit his other siblings. His father was there and invited him to dinner. When they'd finished eating and were clearing the plates, Rodolfo felt the urge to hug him. He was about to do it when he told himself no. Since then he hasn't felt the urge again: he doesn't let it happen.

We meet again in the same café. It's a cold and cloudy day but Rodolfo, who has come from another visit to his nephew in the hospital, is wearing the same black jacket and, underneath, a thin T-shirt.

"My mom left my dad because of me, that's the truth. That's why my mom is so precious to me. She was everything to me. But now, as an adult, I understand my dad. He was sixteen years old, he was a ladies' man, a guitar player. My mom loved him and she gave up everything for him, but before he knew it, the guy had four kids and a fifth on the way. And he must have said: 'No way.' My mom's head is covered in scars and that's unforgivable, but now I don't think that I'm the one who has to do the forgiving."

"Are you mad at him?"

"No."

Rodolfo isn't bitter. He isn't angry. He's not resentful. The nephew in the hospital is the son of his older brother, and he worries about him as much as if he were his own son. His maternal grandfather died of gangrene after a thorn punctured his foot, and Rodolfo still remembers Rubén Carabajal carrying him on his shoulders to the house where the old man lay dying so that he could give him a handkerchief. He was raised in a one-room house that flooded every time it rained, but what he remembers is that it was fun to take cover under the table and play with his friends in the puddles. They didn't have electricity, but he laughs when he recalls how he liked to play with candles. His family couldn't afford to buy new shoes, but he proudly explains how Rubén Carabajal sewed up his old broken shoes and lent Rodolfo his new ones so that he could tear them up playing soccer.

"I had a beautiful childhood. What we suffered most was hunger. Actually, in all the places I've lived I've gone hungry."

The year he chose to move to Buenos Aires to study for a certification in folklore at the IUNA was the worst year in Argentina in recent decades. In December 2001 an economic and social crisis broke out, leaving people dead in the streets, depositors pounding on the doors of banks that had taken their money, and unemployment that reached 21 percent. Rodolfo arrived in February 2002, at age nineteen. Buenos Aires was a city that his parents, aunts, uncles, and friends had never even visited, where there was no work to be had. It was more like a ticking time bomb than a place to call home.

"I was in Santa Rosa, packing my bag to go get on the train, and my dad says to me, 'Son, are you sure you want to go? Listen, we can take care of you here until you find a job.' And I felt the world come crashing down when I heard those words. But I told him, 'No, Dad, I have to go. I want to study.' I went to live in a dorm for students from La Pampa, and from there I walked to the IUNA every day. It was like sixty blocks. The dorm was in the Constitución neighborhood and I had to walk through a rough area, but I didn't have money for the bus. I couldn't find work. Sometimes my mom would send me some credit for the Trueque."

The Trueque Club was an exchange system that flourished in the years after the 2001 crisis because it didn't use money. Participants could swap one item for another or pay for something with credits, which was the currency issued by the club and valid throughout the country.

"But in La Pampa one credit was worth one peso, and here four credits were worth one peso. It was enough to get a pound of sugar. When my mom sent me money, I would save it for bread and sometimes I would buy ground meat. It was hard to have only rice with milk or polenta with milk or flour and milk and then see the person next to you eating a veal steak."

One night he went out with a friend who said, "I'm going to show you Buenos Aires." He took him to Plaza Miserere, the epicenter of Once, a working-class neighborhood where, at night, various elements of the underworld meet. Rodolfo's first nocturnal outing in the city ended with a police officer patting him down against a wall.

"Never in my life had anyone asked me for my identification, I'd never seen a police officer up close, but as soon as they saw us they stopped us and asked for our identification. They saw that my eyes were red, because I'm allergic to smoke, to dust, to the sun, and they thought I was high. They put us up against the wall and started to pat us down. They found my eye drops and that was like a confirmation: 'Ooooh, you're a junkie.' But when I showed them my ID they let us go. I remember that there were some transvestites who said to the cops, 'Hey, buddy, give me a cigarette,' and the cop said, 'Get out of here, get out of here.' I had no idea what was going on. I thought, 'Oh my God, where am I?'"

In time, Rodolfo found work in a factory that made cases for eyeglasses. He also worked at a construction site, where the workers were told to hide when the inspectors arrived, to cover up the fact that the company didn't provide the required protective gear. One day a friend told him that he wanted to introduce him to a great dancer and took him to see the folk-loric dance company called the Rebellion. Rodolfo's friend introduced him to a bald man covered in tattoos and wearing military boots and ripped wide-legged pants, the director of the ballet. Rodolfo said to himself: *This is the great dancer?* The man, Carlos Medina, turned out to be just that, and he soon became one of Rodolfo's close friends. Rodolfo began dancing in the company, where he was partnered with a girl as short as he was and five years his senior. Her name was Miriam Carrizo. He liked her immediately, but she turned him down for eight months straight until finally, after much insistence on his part, they started dating. She moved out of the girls' dorm, he left behind his student housing, and they moved into a house in Pablo Podestá, in the suburbs of Buenos Aires.

"The other day I was sitting at home. I was looking at the living room furniture, and I thought, 'I remember when we bought that and when we bought the stereo.' Every single thing took a huge effort. We would buy something and then we weren't sure if we'd have enough for food. One day in the middle of summer I said to her, '*Negra*, let's go buy a little fan.' We ended up buying a huge turbo fan. When we got home, she said to me, 'Rodo, do you have any money left for food?' And I told her, 'No, do you?' 'No.' And we died laughing. Sometimes we didn't have enough money to take the train into the city. I have some shoes with really slick soles. I'd get Miriam to buy her ticket and I'd start running and then slide under the subway turnstile. One time we each had fifty cents, just enough to take the bus home. But to get to the right bus we had to take the train. And if we paid for the train ticket we wouldn't have had enough to take the bus. Since it was the last train of the night, we got on without paying. We were just approaching our station when the conductor appeared: 'Tickets, kids.' We gave him all the money we had and walked the thirty blocks home from the train station at one o'clock in the morning. But that's not so painful. What does hurt is when you don't have enough to buy food. To get home with her and see that you don't have anything, and see her crying because she's so hungry. That hurts."

After Rodolfo graduated, he started teaching at the IUNA. He got some private students as well as some dance classes at elementary schools outside the city. This has given him some—but not much—stability.

———————

He likes to read but he's only recently had enough money for books in the last few years. Since then, he's read the complete works of Shakespeare, *The Iliad* (thanks to which he learned about Achilles's heel), *The Odyssey*, and *Oedipus Rex* (which taught him enough about the Oedipus complex to conclude that he'd never had it). He doesn't have the internet at home and he's not used to sending e-mails, but his text messages have perfect syntax. One, from June 2011, says, "Hello, Leila, could you send me your e-mail address? I need to ask you a question." Another, from July: "Hello, Leila, we saw each other last Saturday and I've been worried about you. I hope things are going well." He's always searching for the lesson in anything you tell him. One day he told me that he'd been invited to give classes in a city far away. When I asked him if he'd made the trip by plane or bus, he told me he went by bus. I said that now that he's the runner-up, maybe he could negotiate better conditions. Months later, we were talking by telephone and he told me that he'd made a decision about a certain job: "You told me I can negotiate better conditions now." He has an excellent memory and he's full of gratitude. He saved the poem that the cultural director of Guatraché wrote after seeing him dance for the first time: it still makes him emotional. It saddens him to see that in big cities parents work so many hours and only see their children after they're already asleep. He prays before going to bed, goes to Mass, says with feeling, "Thank God"—"My parents are healthy, thank God," "I have a lot of work, thank God"—but he vehemently opposes the dogmatic vision of the Church and refuses to participate in religious ceremonies ordained by priests who "still believe that God is going to punish you if you don't go to Mass." He couldn't go on the graduation trip with his classmates because he didn't have the money, but he's grateful that through dance he's had the opportunity to see places like Bariloche that, on his own, he would never have been able to visit. He tells a story like any good storyteller: he takes his time, knows how to generate suspense, and imitates the protagonists perfectly, like his friend who fell into a ditch hunting *peludos*—a kind of small armadillo—in La Pampa. He's stubborn and ethical. He once called the factory where he always bought his boots and told them he needed a pair by a certain date. They told him that the boots wouldn't be ready until December 15. He needed them sooner and asked if they could do it as a favor. They told him they couldn't. So he bought them somewhere else. Two weeks later the first factory called to tell him that another malambo dancer hadn't come to pick up his boots and that, if he wanted them, they were available. At first Rodolfo thought about trying to sell the ones he'd just bought. But immediately after, he decided that, since they'd refused the favor when he needed it, he shouldn't buy the boots from them now. So he said no thanks, and he got used to his new boots (which wasn't easy, because they had square toes and he'd always danced with round-toed boots). When he speaks with someone younger, or someone he cares for, he calls them "Pa," "Papi," or "Papito," and he uses the formal *usted* address for anyone even ten years older, unless he knows them very well. In 2009 he spent a few days in Santa Rosa. A neighbor offered him a job in the fields, and since he was totally broke, he accepted. The job consisted of shoveling up wheat that had fallen to the sides of the combine harvester and throwing it back into the mouth of the combine so that nothing was wasted. It was ten hours walking in infernal heat beside a weathered old man—Uncle Ramón—who never complained once, and so Rodolfo, out of pride, followed his example. Although he swears it was the worst job of his life, he tells it like a fun adventure. He believes that politicians, whether on the right or on the left, don't really have the best interest of the poor in mind and that "at best, they give us what we need sometimes, but they never teach us how to get what we need ourselves, so that they'll always have us by the balls." He's read most of Che Guevara's writings and says that, while he's not active in any party, he's touched by "that asthmatic doctor who had the courage to do what he did."

In 2011, a typical day in the life of Rodolfo proceeds as follows: he wakes at six a.m., eats breakfast, travels an hour and a half to San Fernando, where his coach Fernando Castro lives, and trains for two hours. On Tuesdays and Thursdays he goes from there to a school in Laferrere, where he teaches music to kids in first and third grades; from Laferrere he travels to González Catán, where he gives classes from six to nine at night to a folkloric dance company. His trip home takes two and a half hours using three different forms of transport. On Wednesdays and Fridays he gives classes at the IUNA until four p.m. and then at a dance company in Benavídez, a suburb on the other side of town, until nine at night. On Sundays and Mondays he teaches group folkloric dance lessons in Merlo and Dorrego. San Fernando, Laferrere, González Catán, Merlo, Dorrego, Benavídez: all these places are very far from where he lives and also far from one another, spread out around an urban conglomeration infamous for its violence: Greater Buenos Aires, home to twenty-two million people, maybe more.

"From Fernando's house I take bus number 21 to Liniers, and from there the 218 to Laferrere, to go to the elementary school. When I finish at the school, I take the 218 to González Catán, where the dance company is. To get back home I take the 218 to Liniers and then the 237 from there. But if I have enough change on me, I go to the San Justo traffic circle and take the Costera Express bus, then I get off at Márques and Perón, and from there I take the 169 home. The other day in Benavídez I got off work really late, at like ten, and at that time it's dangerous to leave the neighborhood, so I had to stay the night at the house where I give the classes. Sometimes my teacher friends say to me, 'Why do you go teach those kids who just get into drugs as soon as they get out of school?' And

I tell them that maybe there's a kid who comes out of my class and becomes a musician. Who knows?"

———————

It's June, the middle of the Argentinian winter. It's ten in the morning, and at his house in Pablo Podestá, Rodolfo serves maté. He's set out toast, *dulce de leche*, and butter on a tray in the living room. The house belongs to Miriam's parents. Her father, a retired employee of the YPF oil company, and his wife, a tailor, live in Caleta Olivia, a small town in Patagonia. They have a yard with fruit trees, two bedrooms, a bathroom, all freshly painted.

"We painted it ourselves. If we don't do it ourselves, it costs a fortune."

In the kitchen, there's a picture of Jesus: JESUS BELIEVES IN YOU. In the living room, a framed picture of the couple with the caption FOR AN ETERNAL LIFE TOGETHER.

"Before, you could see a cement mixer in the background of the picture. But I went to a photo shop and the guy erased the mixer and painted in a blue background. It turned out nice."

"Is the neighborhood quiet?"

"Yes, things happen, but it's quiet, thank God."

The year they moved there, they watched as a motorcycle turned the corner at full speed and the driver fired three shots into their neighbor, leaving him dead on the sidewalk. Miriam and Rodolfo only dared turn off their lights, and they remained silent as the motorcycle took off.

"His wife was screaming, 'They killed my husband, they

65

killed my husband.' But we're all alone here, we don't have any family. So we just stayed still."

Rodolfo opens his computer and looks for some videos that he's gathered to teach me how to distinguish errors and excessive movements in malambo routines.

"The malambo has slow parts, medium parts, fast parts. It starts slow, and then it speeds up. As it speeds up, your chances to show off movement are fewer, but you can show more quality. From the slow part to the medium part you have to show a change in attitude, and in the last part you have to close your eyes, say 'God help me,' and really move your legs. Look at this guy's shoulders. See how they go up? You have to avoid that. Your shoulders shouldn't go up. Now people are starting to shout and applaud and you can see it on his face: he starts smiling. The idea is that you don't let the people build you up, but that you build the people up. And see his breathing, how he's panting? You have to avoid that. When you land the final stomp of the malambo, you sink into the floor, to plant yourself firmly, your torso raised, always breathing through your nose. If you breathe through your mouth, it's over, it gets impossible to control, you can't breathe and everyone can see that you're tired, like this kid. Breathing through your nose keeps you calm, so that no one knows. No one should ever know what's going on inside you."

No one should ever know what's going on inside you.

———

One day, on the way to the IUNA, he tells me about a dream he says he will never forget. He walked from a sand dune down to the edge of the sea, and when he was on the beach the sea started to rise. He tried to get back to the dune but couldn't. He asked for help from a person on top of the dune, and the person said, "No, you can do it." He kept trying, until finally he stepped onto solid rock and was able to get up on the dune. From the top, he could see a huge city. He jumped over a barbed-wire fence and he was in the city. He thinks that the person on the dune was God.

"And it's incredible. After that I went to read the Bible, and there it said that God is the rock on which we all stand."

Rodolfo walks quickly and silently; he seems tense, like he's worried about things he has to do. Suddenly he says, "The hardest thing for me is to get onstage and say: 'This is mine.'"

"Why?"

"Because it's enormous. And I'm afraid of enormity. I'm terrified of things that have no end in sight. Only last year could I finally look at the ocean. Stand in front of the ocean and look at its enormity and not be afraid."

———

Things that would seem childish to some people he finds hilarious: he tells the story of Gonzalo "Pony" Molina, fellow dancer and now a friend of his, who wrote on Facebook, "I have something to tell you, I'm going to be a dad." The next day, after receiving dozens of congratulations, Pony wrote, "My dog is pregnant." Rodolfo thinks the joke is infinitely funny. I, on the other hand, must look like an imbecile to him asking the same question over and over: why put in so much effort to win at a festival known to so few people and which, at the same time, means the end of your career? I want to say, without saying it, that being famous to a few thousand people doesn't seem like something worth sacrificing everything for. He is patient with me, trying to explain, over and over, the same thing:

"Being the champion at Laborde has huge value for a very small circle of people, but for us it's the ultimate glory. The year you're the champion you get asked to be photographed all the time, do interviews, sign autographs. And it's up to you to take advantage of it, because afterward you're not going to use your legs anymore. Once your legs are used up, you have to start using other tools. Laborde gives you the chance to become a real, proper man. Not a guy who wants to win to pick up girls or to show everyone that he's better, but to prove that if you work hard, silently, humbly, you can do anything. That's why I'd like God to grant me maturity, to help me become a man, to make it to Laborde and leave everything there. Laborde had me hooked from the first time I set foot onstage. And if it's God's will for Laborde, the ultimate glory, to take your career, that's fine. It gives you the maximum honor, and then it takes everything. But it's not that I want to be champion just to secure my economic future or to see my face on a poster. I want to be champion because I've wanted to be the champion since I was twelve years old. To finish my career there would be amazing."

I always nod and agree with him. But deep down, I still wonder how it's possible that such an unknown prize could make someone say what this man keeps telling me over and over: that he'll march, happily, to his martyrdom.

Rac-tac-tac, rac-tac-tac, rac-tac-tac.

It's an afternoon in June and Rodolfo is giving a class at the IUNA. The room is large with a wooden floor, mirrors, a piano. The students look like the twenty-first-century version of *Fame*, girls and boys dressed in all kinds of headbands, sweatpants, leggings, leotards, colorful leg warmers. Rodolfo wears jeans with the cuffs turned up, a black T-shirt, sneakers.

"Watch your facial expression," he says. "If you're going like this, it doesn't make sense to be smiling."

When he says "like this" he stomps like someone trying to bring down a building. Although some students try to imitate him, it requires great effort and artifice to do what for Rodolfo is a natural gesture.

"Come on, come on. This is what you chose to do. Higher. *Rac-tac-tac, rac-tac-tac, rac-tac-tac.*"

Rodolfo is discreet. He doesn't speak negatively of his competitors, and if he ever mentions someone by name, it's only to speak well of them: so-and-so is wise, or no one moves their feet as well as such and such instructor. That's why it seems strange to me when one day in the café, he mentions the name of the Laborde champion he met on a judges' panel. Rodolfo asked him for advice on what to correct from his 2011 presentation.

"He told me, 'Look, do your best, but it's not going to be easy, because you also have the runner-up, Pony, from La Pampa, who's the favorite for champion. You can be totally prepared, but when you're backstage and you hear your name and you have to go on, your ass fills up with doubt.' And I told him, 'Oh, okay, thanks.' And the next week I went to the Garrahan Children's Hospital to donate blood for a little boy whose school I teach at. You go in there and you see those sick little kids and that's where your ass really fills up with doubts. For me, being champion at Laborde is a huge dream. But if I don't win, I don't win. And I don't want to be a guy who can move his legs fast but then can't even string two words together. If I don't win at Laborde, I'll keep going to the schools, to the IUNA. But I know where it is that my ass really fills up with doubts. And it's not in Laborde."

He almost never says words like "ass." When he does, his face shows great distaste and he looks down to hide feelings that, I suppose, he doesn't want anyone to see.

———————

"Rodo is what you see. He's super transparent."

Miriam Carrizo, Rodolfo's wife, studied to become a folkloric dance instructor. Although she's five years older than he is, she looks much younger, with her smooth dark skin and sweet voice like a little girl's. Rodolfo loves her and he fears her, because she's able to tell him what no one else would dare: that he danced badly, that he wasn't focused, that he lacked attitude.

"Rodo never gets mad, not even if the sky falls down on top of him. He's very calm, very peaceful, very diplomatic. Maybe he'll get mad, but he'll tell you everything in a very respect-ful way. And for him, Laborde is very important. I've been through everything with him. We had to give up a million things, go without things to be able to buy a pair of boots. He leaves home at seven in the morning and comes back at midnight, and I'm praying that nothing happens to him. Or in-stead of relaxing on Sunday, I go with him to the track to run."

"Does all that bother you?"

"Not at all. It's his dream and I know that if he wins it's going to be the happiest moment of his life. Of our life."

———————

All through 2011, Rodolfo trained every day, practiced his malambo routine up to twelve times, ran for an hour and a half, jumped rope, went to the gym. He watched what he ate. He lost weight. And in the first week in January he went to Laborde to try for the title of champion.

Cecilia Lorenc Valcarce, the festival's press director, said in the e-mail she sent me on December 27, 2011, "The Festival is

71

from the tenth to the fifteenth (the early morning of the sixteenth). Rodolfo, as the runner-up, competes in the first slot on the first night (it's the perk of being runner-up)." So from Tuesday the tenth to midday Sunday the fifteenth, Rodolfo would have to stay in Laborde, not knowing whether or not he would make it to the finals. And I, of course, would be with him.

———————

"Hello, Rodolfo, it's Leila."

"Hello, Leila, how are you?"

"Good. You?"

"Good, thank God. I'm on the bus. I'm going to Río Cuarto and from there I'm taking another bus to Laborde."

"Is your family going?"

"Yes, everyone is going. My dad, my mom, my brother Diego, Chiri, the kids, my sister-in-law's sister."

"Are they already there?"

"No, they're going next week ..."

"And where are they staying?"

"They rented a bus that holds forty-five people. Because they couldn't afford to stay at the campground, it's too expensive, so they borrowed some money and rented that. They're going to sleep there, on the bus."

On the other end of the line, Rodolfo sounds like he's riding in a convertible with the top down, radiant and triumphant.

———————

In the summer of 2012 Argentina is suffering an extreme drought, but the south of the province of Córdoba is all green fields. Dust floats in the air, coloring everything in a surreal light. On Monday, January 9, one day before the start of the festival, with temperatures around 113 degrees Fahrenheit, the town of Laborde has a power outage at one in the afternoon. When I call Rodolfo from Buenos Aires to ask him how he was, he says, "Cold," and starts laughing. He is staying in a rented house with some friends who have traveled to Laborde to support him.

"Are you okay?"

"Yes, I'm okay, thank God."

On Tuesday, January 10, Rodolfo is scheduled to dance. That afternoon, I am traveling to Laborde by car. At five o'clock, before I reach a town called Firmat, a huge storm erupts. First the wind whips up a blinding curtain of dust, then an impenetrable rain is unleashed. I seek refuge under the awning of a building on the side of the road. That's where I was when the festival's publicity director, Cecilia Lorenc Valcarce, sent me a message. "Where are you? The committee is meeting to decide whether to cancel. Major winds. Things flying everywhere." An hour later, already back on the road, I receive another message from Cecilia: "Malambo all canceled until tomorrow."

I think of Rodolfo and I think of this unexpected cancellation. I wonder if this change—in a universe where any tiny detail can have devastating effects on a competitor's composure—can hurt his chances. I send him a message, but he doesn't respond. At eight o'clock that night I make it to Monte Maíz, a town twenty kilometers from Laborde. I am there because in Laborde there are no vacancies.

On Wednesday morning, the anxieties I felt Tuesday on the highway persist and multiply. Now I'm concerned that it might be disconcerting for Rodolfo to have a journalist following his every move. In that extremely controlled atmosphere surrounding every hopeful before the competition, I could be the equivalent of a huge toxic bacteria. An interference. Does Rodolfo know that his story is just as important, even if he doesn't end up becoming the next champion? But *is* his story just as important even if he doesn't end up becoming the next champion? At ten in the morning, I call and ask if I can come over to his house to start working.

"Of course, *negra,* come on over."

At midday, despite yesterday's storm, or maybe because of it, Laborde sails under clear blue skies. The house where Rodolfo is staying is on the corner of Estrada and Avellaneda. He shares it with Álvaro Melián, one of his students; some friends from the Rebellion dance company—Luis, Jonathan, Noelia, Priscilla, Diana—who traveled here to support him; and Carlos Medina. They are also expecting, in a few days, Miriam's brother, sister-in-law, and niece, Javier, Graciela, and Chiara, as well as Tonchi, a childhood friend. Miriam, who dances in the opening of the festival, can't stay in the house because of insurance issues with the dance company she belongs to. Rodolfo's parents, his siblings Diego and Chiri, his nieces and nephews, his sister-in-law's sister, her kids, and her husband are all staying in the bus they rented, parked on the edge of the campground. The house is large. It has a kitchen, two bedrooms, a living room, a bathroom, and a backyard. There are traces everywhere of the people who own the house: decorations, glassware, clothes in the closets. Rodolfo and Fernando Castro wipe dirt off the table in the patio.

"Have a seat, *negra*, we'll have some matés. We just got here."

Rodolfo just got back from Mass and he's wearing a shirt that says NO MORE VIOLENCE/THIS IS A MESSAGE FROM GOD. This year, he'll be accompanied by Fernando Castro on guitar and Pony on bass drum, meaning he'll go onstage flanked by champions. He'll wear the same blue suit he wore last year for the northern style, but for the southern style he has changed his entire outfit. His sister gave him the hat, the vest was embroidered by a group of students from the IUNA, the tie he'll wear was given to him by Pony (it's the same one Pony wore when he was named champion), a friend's father gave him his jacket, the boots and the poncho (dark, with red and brown embroidery) were lent to him, the *rastra* (decorated with his initials: R.G.A.) was given as a gift by Carlos Medina (who in addition to being a dancer is also an artist), and the *cribo* was given to him by a woman in Santa Rosa.

"But the white shirt is mine," he says, laughing, as he sews a chin strap—a strip of braided leather—onto his hat using a thick needle and the help of a clothespin. "The old one fell apart after being soaked in sweat too many times. They wanted to charge me like 150 pesos to fix it here. Luckily I'd brought this needle."

Carlos Medina, a talkative man who always seems to be in a

good mood and wears a baseball cap day or night, serves maté and says that when he was making the *rastra*, he asked Rodolfo to give him the initials of his name.

"He gave me like forty-five letters. Luis Rodolfo Antonio such and such so-and-so. I told him, 'Dude, just give me three letters or it's going to look more like a miniskirt than a belt.'"

At another table under a tree, some young kids are painting a banner that reads:

> *You'll show them who you are*
> *They'll see what you're made of*
> *That what you have in your heart*
> *Brought you where you are today*
> *Let's go Rodo!*

———————

The verse paraphrases a reggaeton song by Don Omar that Rodolfo always listens to: "I'll show them who I am, they'll see what I'm made of, what I carry in my heart brought me to where I am./And they'll see me triumph and be the champion, the one who didn't win the prize will be crowned the king."

"Did the storm catch you on the highway?" Rodolfo asks.

"Yes. I had to stop."

"Here, things were flying everywhere. The wind blew away a ton of tents in the campground, but my parents, thank God, were really comfortable in the bus."

I ask myself how comfortable they could be with ten people on a bus, no beds, and an improvised bathroom, but I say, "That's great."

———————

Lunch for the teams is served at the Laborde Athletic and Cultural Recreation Club. Every day at noon people sing and dance while others eat and shout as an impromptu dance takes place, unofficially called the cafeteria *peña*. But it's late now and the huge room is empty. The long tables are covered with dirty plates and cups, and a man cleans up using an ingenious method: rolling up the paper tablecloths into a huge bundle of plates, cups, and scraps. There are three people in the kitchen. I approach them and ask, "Is there anything left to eat?"

"Yes, just have a seat."

I sit at one of the tables over a bowl of noodle stew, and a tall man with dark hair asks if he can join me.

"Of course."

The man has the austere tidiness of country folk, and he starts up a conversation in the same easy manner with which, in a room containing hundreds of empty tables and chairs, he asked to sit next to me.

"I've been the representative from my province, Río Negro, for thirty-seven years. Things have changed, for good and bad. Before, you would see a kid from Corrientes dance malambo and you knew he was from Corrientes, one from Buenos Aires and the same thing. Now, because the champions travel all around the country, training this one or that one, everyone ends up dancing the same. And it's all very athletic. Sometimes you see them dance and they look like machines. But I admire their effort, because they're very humble kids that spend a lot of money to prepare themselves, and there are no guarantees they're going to win. Of course, if they become the champion, they're set for life. They can earn a hundred dollars per class, or more, and ciao."

Before he stands up to go take his siesta, I ask him his name. He says: "Arnaldo Pérez. Good-bye."

Arnaldo Pérez. The 1976 champion from Río Negro. His coach didn't know how to dance malambo but was a historian who, after seeing the dance at an interprovince competition, offered to give him classes, traveling 250 kilometers over dirt roads every two weeks to where Arnaldo lived. He never accepted a single peso for the lessons. Arnaldo Pérez is also a member of the judges' panel this year. During our conversation, before I knew who he was, I asked him if he liked, as a candidate for champion, Rodolfo González Alcántara, last year's runner-up. He answered that honestly, he didn't.

———————

It's Wednesday, midnight. Backstage, as if a year hasn't passed, the same Carnival-esque chaos reigns: the same women in wispy dresses, the same serious tiny children, the same faces— Sebastián Sayago, who's competing again and dances tonight, Hugo Moreyra, Ariel Ávalos, Hernán Villagra. The champions return, year after year, not only because that's what's expected of them, but also because they love to be there and because they train hopefuls in diverse categories. Someone's painted the word MALAMBO in flour on the mirror fixed to the wall. The announcer's voice says, "And so, ladies and gentlemen, the nation, that was the junior malambo quartets! In those kids we see the hope and hard work of every coach, every parent! They are the seeds of future champions!"

The junior malambo category includes kids from ten to thirteen years old. The maximum time stipulated for the category is three minutes. When they finish dancing, the pre-teen dancers usually throw themselves into the arms of their coaches and sob uncontrollably as the adults, filled with pride, tell them, "Cry, cry, that's what you should be feeling." Now, backstage, there are several of these kids bawling their eyes out in the arms of their trainers.

It's twelve fifteen a.m. but Rodolfo has been in dressing room 4 since eleven. He takes off his T-shirt, his pants, his sneakers. He pulls out a bottle of water and his dance attire from his brown bag. He puts on his shirt, *cribo*, horsehide boots, *chiripá*, and sash. Fernando Castro, already dressed in his gaucho attire, watches him in silence and, with the same imperturbable patience as the previous year, makes sure the folds of the poncho are even, the embroidery lines up. At twelve thirty, Rodolfo begins pacing like a caged and rabid tiger. Then he wets his hair, opens his backpack, takes out the Bible, reads, whispers, puts it away, takes out his cell phone, and the Almafuerte song "Be You" begins to play. Fernando Castro, with the guitar in his lap, says to him quietly, "We're going to win, partner. Bring out your ambition, your happiness."

Rodolfo nods his head in agreement, mute.

"Come on—attitude. Get the blood flowing. Bring it, bring it, bring it."

Rodolfo nods without stopping his movement. Then, like last year, Fernando gets up, leaves, and we're left alone. And I tell myself that I shouldn't stay there, but I stay.

At one a.m. the Laborde hymn plays—"Dance the malambo"— and the voice of the announcer says, "Ladies and gentlemen, the time has arrived for the category we've all been waiting for—in Laborde, and in all of Argentina!"

When the fireworks go off, Rodolfo lifts his head and puts on his hat. His face is that of a stone idol, the face of another person.

"Ladies and gentlemen of the jury, champions, we are going to present the main malambo category!"

Rodolfo opens the door of the dressing room and walks to the stage. He stands between the curtains, his legs apart, his back stiff like someone ready to kill.

"We present now a man hailing from the province of La Pampa! With our hearts ablaze, and with fiery applause, we welcome the 2011 main malambo runner-up, *Rooodooolfo Gonzáaalez Aaaalcántaraaa!*"

The audience explodes. There are shouts: "Bravo!" "Come on, Rodo!" "You can do it!" "Come, on, macho!" I pick out Miriam's voice among them. Rodolfo, still behind the curtain, makes the sign of the cross.

And he goes onstage.

Fernando Castro's guitar sounds like a storm of threats, like a warning. It sounds like an avalanche, a rockslide, thunder: like the last day on Earth. Rodolfo enters the stage from one side. He takes a few steps and stops to measure the magnitude of his task. Then he walks to the center and moves toward the audience with three silent steps, like an animal on the hunt. And he freezes, with his legs wide, his arms at his sides, his fingers tensed. The guitar peels off a round chord, loud and clear, and Rodolfo lets two blows fall onto the wood: *tac tac.* And from that moment, the malambo takes place somewhere between earth and sky. Rodolfo's legs look like flaming eagles, and lost somewhere beyond this world, fatally handsome, tall as a tree, clear as the smell of jasmine, he raises himself brutally over the filigree of his toes, he shatters, kicks, roars with the cunning of a feline, slides with the grace of a deer, he is mountain and avalanche, sea and foam. Then, at the end, he slams a foot into the boards and remains still, serene and clean, as frightening as a storm of blood. With an arrogant gesture, he straightens his jacket—as though saying it was no big deal—and leaning forward in reverence, he touches his hat with the tip of a finger, turns halfway around, and leaves the stage.

"Time employed: four minutes forty-five seconds," says the woman's distant, impassive voice.

I run backstage and what I see there is total destruction. Rodolfo and Fernando embrace in silence, like two men in mourning. Carlos Medina's eyes are full of tears, and Miriam Carrizo, hugging him, sobs uncontrollably. I think something must have gone wrong with the dance and I hadn't been able to tell. But then Rodolfo takes off his hat, huffs, and Miriam goes to him, hugs him, and says, "Rodo, it was beautiful, it was great."

Carlos Medina, who can hardly breathe, looks at me.

"I've never seen anyone dance like that," he says.

A few meters away, in the doorway of his dressing room, Sebastián Sayago, who will dance in a few minutes, prays.

It's almost two in the morning when Sebastián Sayago leaves the stage shouting, "Shit, Goddamn it, shit!"

His companions surround him and tell him, "Get it out, good, get it out," but Sebastián is furious and wears an expression of pain. They bring him water. Rodolfo and Fernando greet him, and he disappears soon after.

Rodolfo enters his dressing room, takes off his jacket, vest, *rastra*. He leaves on only the *cribo* and shirt and the loose white clothing gives him the look of a penitent or altar boy. One by one, the hopefuls go onstage, from Buenos Aires, San Luis, La Rioja. Outside the dressing room, the girls from a provincial team form a circle and recite, in unison:

"*Streeetch, dooown, streeetch, uuup.*"

And they stretch, bend down, stretch, rise.

Rodolfo drinks water, takes off his shirt and *cribo*, and begins to get dressed to dance the return, the northern style. Once dressed, he leaves the dressing room and goes through his entire malambo in front of the mirror on the wall. All around, people watch in silence. Then he returns to the dressing room and I stay outside, taking notes next to a boy dressed as a gaucho who checks messages on a cell phone. A few minutes later, the red-haired man who announces the order of the performances runs by, shouting, "La Pampa! La Pampa! Where is La Pampa?"

Since no one answers, I say, "In dressing room 4."

The redhead takes off, bangs on the door of Rodolfo's dressing room, and shouts.

"La Pampa is next for the main malambo!"

A last-minute change: according to the program, Rodolfo should go on in a half hour, and this change, I imagine, must take him by surprise. But a provincial delegation still dances onstage, and I tell myself that it won't be a problem, there's time. Then I see Miriam walk by with her cell phone in her hand and an expression of extreme distress, and I know something's terribly wrong.

"What happened?"

"Pony—we can't find him anywhere and he has to play the drum with Rodo!"

Miriam tries calling Pony, but he could be anywhere: eating pizza, giving an interview, signing autographs. And to hear a cell phone, in that crowd, with all the music playing, is almost impossible.

Rodolfo asks, "What's wrong?"

"We can't find Pony," says Miriam, and she dials again.

I think, "How terrible!" But I don't know if I'm thinking about him, or me, or both.

Just like in the movies, three minutes before Rodolfo is to go onstage Pony appears. Miriam is furious with the festival organizers, but Rodolfo puts on his hat and leaves the dressing room without a word. I watch him approach the stage, and with his back to me he makes the sign of the cross. I think that if in 2011 he was distracted when his vest snagged on his jacket, the stress of this last-minute scare could have disastrous effects. As I think these things, Rodolfo goes onstage and dances. When he finishes, the distant, impassive female voice says:

"Time employed: four minutes, thirty-two seconds."

Rodolfo leaves the stage upset and goes straight into the dressing room. Miriam follows. She stares at him without saying a word, her forehead creased, as if she were trying to solve some secret message. When Rodolfo catches his breath, she tells him that he didn't dance as well as she'd expected, that she didn't like the first two figures, that they didn't look good. Rodolfo says that yes, he already knows, that he's not happy with it, that the music didn't follow him, that he left the stage knowing that he hadn't given everything, that the schedule change had made him nervous and he hadn't had time to concentrate before going on. He takes off his jacket and boots and leaves the dressing room. Outside, many people come up to hug him, to wish him luck. A young boy says he has something for him. He puts his hand in his pocket, takes out an object, and gives it to him.

"Here, it was my grandmother's."

It's a rosary. Rodolfo thanks him, kisses it, and hangs it around his neck.

The first news I get the next day is that Sebastián Sayago injured himself while dancing and is now getting injections in case he moves on to the finals. The second piece of news—a rumor—is that the judges were very impressed with Rodolfo's dancing. Then I meet with Rodolfo, and he tells me that he watched the video of yesterday's northern malambo and he looked better than he'd thought, so he is more relaxed now.

"Want to come to the campground to see my parents?" he asks me.

"Okay."

A bus that reads ARIEL TOURS is parked outside the campground, a green space full of tents on the other side of Route 11. Rodolfo's parents, siblings, and other relatives sleep in the faded orange bus, but they spend the day on the campground for a minimal fee that gives them access to the grills, pool, showers, and toilets. Rubén Carabajal is a dark, round man with a thin beard and mustache. He hardly speaks at all. María Luisa Alcántara is short, shorter than Rodolfo, very thin, with delicate, squarish features and small, sad eyes; she looks like she's perpetually on the verge of falling asleep. Arthritis has left knobs on her knees and hands.

"Rodo is so good and responsible. An excellent son, thank God," she says, seated on a cement bench in front of a table set with maté and cookies. "He was very sick when he was little, with pneumonia. He was in the hospital all the time. I stayed with him, and I had to wash clothes in the hospital room, so I hung the clothes in the little bathroom. And the nurse asked me, 'Hey, González, don't you have any family?' Yes, I told her, but they don't come to see me. Only one time they came to see me, when they'd given Rodolfo an hour left to live. The only one who came to see me was Rubén, who would ask to donate blood and then stay. We've been through a lot together. That's why, when Rodo told me he was going to Buenos Aires, I wanted to die. He went when things were at their worst. But he said to me, 'Mom, I have to go, because I'm not going to make anything of myself here.' I had a little nephew who was killed by a gunshot seven years ago. And he said, 'The only cousin with real balls is Rodolfo, who moved to Buenos Aires at nineteen without knowing anyone there.'"

"That nephew was killed?"

"Yes, one block from my house. My neighborhood is infamous. It's called Mataderos, which means *slaughterhouse*. On the GPS it says 'dangerous area.'"

"When Rodolfo left, we didn't have a peso to give him," says Rubén Carabajal. "The situation was terrible. Now I work for the city, doing maintenance, and we earn a little. But at that time I made 150 pesos. Nothing."

"You never thought Rodolfo should study something more practical than dance?"

"No, that was his dream," María Luisa says. "To have a son who's a national champion is a big deal. He said, 'Mom, I'm doing something I like.' I told him, 'Okay, son, you have to be happy.' We always support him in everything. When he comes to Santa Rosa, in 100-degree heat, he goes out to run ten kilometers. He doesn't have a platform at his house in Buenos Aires, so he has to tap on the cement, with his horsehide boots. Do you know how that must hurt? Poor thing, he works so hard. Sometimes I call him at twelve thirty at night and he's not even home from work yet, he's waiting for the train to go home."

The conversation turns to family stories: the day that María Luisa told Rodolfo, because he always got beaten up at school, "If you don't hit all of them next time, when you come home I'm going to hit you." The time that Rubén stole a pig because they didn't have enough to eat, and ended up in jail. The armadillo hunts that the men of the family frequently undertake.

"Last time, they came back with twenty-five armadillos," says María Luisa. "At one point my house looked like a zoo. We had otters, lapwings, geese, an ostrich. A little fox. One day the ostrich escaped and the neighbors ate him."

"How did you know it was the neighbors?"

"Because the lady herself came and told me that they'd found an ostrich and they'd eaten it."

Last year María Luisa had to have spinal surgery in Buenos Aires, a disc replacement. They now have huge medical bills because their health insurance covered everything but the hospital stay.

"And we have to pay back the money we borrowed for the bus. A neighbor lent us part of it and Chiri's husband the rest. Right, Chiri?"

Chiri works as a housekeeper and her husband is a garbage collector, a job that, in Argentina, is reasonably well paid. As she fumbles with the baby, Chiri says, "First you have to pay the neighbor. Then we'll see."

María Luisa makes a face that says, "What can I do?"

"I believe that God will help us come out all right," she says.

"Are you staying for the barbeque?" asks Rubén. "We already put on some meat for you."

"Laborde has made you reevaluate certain things, personal reflections, it's marked a shift in your career."

"Yes, Laborde brings out other things. When you're up on the stage you have to leave many emotions there. For me it's all been a huge learning experience, it's been a breakthrough, a before and after."

"Well, the best of luck. We hope to see you onstage after four in the morning on Sunday, Rodolfo."

"Thank you and hello to all my loved ones."

"We were just speaking with Rodolfo González Alcántara, one of the most serious and thoughtful runners-up we've seen. He spoke to us about a breakthrough, and he's figured out how to make the most of every situation, learning from every lesson."

I'm driving in the car listening to an interview with Rodolfo on the local radio. He often speaks this way, he's so polite and vague, and you want to ask him where it is, where he keeps the monster that consumes him when he goes onstage. Where is he hiding it?

———

Thursday night there's a huge moon. The hopeful from Tucumán leaves the stage blind with emotion, and he walks into the wrong dressing room. That's all.

———

On Friday morning, Héctor Aricó walks by the spot on the field where the main malambo hopefuls are taking a group photo.

"What an ugly bunch," he jokes.

A crowd of children frame the shot with their cell phones. I realize that Rodolfo is the shortest of all.

———

At six in the evening on Friday, Álvaro Melián, Rodolfo's student, sits on a windowsill, silently taking in the scene. Fernando Castro, on a sofa covered in clothes, holds his guitar between his knees. Rodolfo is in the middle of the empty living room, dressed in his *cribo*, *chiripá*, and a blue T-shirt. Yesterday one of his molars started hurting and he has a swollen ankle. He went to the Laborde Hospital, where they proposed an anti-inflammatory injection and painkiller, but he refused out of fear that it might affect his dancing. His mother said she could give him some painkillers and anti-inflammatory pills, but when he went to pick them up he found Rubén, in the suffocating heat, sleeping in the aisle of the bus, and his mother doing the same in one of the seats, her neck twisted awkwardly. I found out later that the scene had made his stomach turn.

"It's unbelievable," he says now, complaining about a figure that he can't quite get right. "I'm counting from this beat but it's from that beat."

Fernando Castro looks at him and strums the guitar without saying a word. Rodolfo practices the figure again and again. Sometimes he stops, and then Fernando speaks as if he were trying to hypnotize him.

"Think about what it cost for you to be here. Try to imagine that you're in the finals. Think about how you've fought. Think about the emotion, the adrenaline. Think about the moment when they say your name and you go onstage. At first you just give as much as needed. Then you end it with all your heart and all your strength. Imagine that everything else is in slow motion and you're going superfast. Now, come on—from your entrance."

Rodolfo leaves the room and comes back in, shooting sparks from his eyes. The bare soles of his feet sound like the crack of a whip against the floor.

"Feel that you are the champion, damn it!" Fernando shouts.

Rodolfo goes through his entire malambo, but he's not happy with it. When he finishes, he says, "It's the first rehearsal since I danced, and I'm starting to feel pains that I didn't even know I had. Tomorrow I want to have a good rehearsal, because this one was shit."

————————

Saturday morning his childhood friend Tonchi arrives. And even though it's a nerve-wracking time—the day before the names of the finalists are announced—Rodolfo's rehearsal goes perfectly. Then he has pasta for lunch, gets phone calls of encouragement from friends, he rests, sleeps.

————————

On Sunday morning I try to reach Rodolfo but I can't. At 11:20 he answers his phone to tell me he's at Mass.

At the church there are several girls dressed as *paisanas* and some men dressed as gauchos. Rodolfo wears a white shirt and track pants, and he's sitting on a pew next to Miriam and Tonchi, a young man, dark and short. Rodolfo, with his head bent, files into the line to receive communion at the altar. Soon afterward the priest announces that Mass has ended and he asks for a warm applause for the participants of the festival.

"*Viva la Argentina!*" he says.

"*Viva!*" responds the crowd, with a shout that makes the stainedglass windows rattle.

Then we go home.

———————————

Tonchi's real name is Gastón and he's been dancing malambo since he was little.

"I danced jazz tango. I have the Grammy winner Paquito D'Riviera's costume from the *Xuxa* TV variety show. I played Paquito in a show at school."

Tonchi and Rodolfo are sitting in the backyard drinking maté, and for a while they seem to forget why we're all there: to wait for the call from the representative of La Pampa, who will let Rodolfo know if he's made it to the finals.

"When I first saw this guy in the Mamüll dance group, I wasn't sure about him," says Rodolfo. "We didn't even say hello to each other. Then we started dancing together, two of my cousins and him. The four midgets. I was chubby, a little jug. And we were so annoying."

"When we showed up at the competition in Bahía Blanca they almost ran us out of there," says Tonchi. "We picked a bunch of unripe lemons, and we would hide and throw lemons at people."

"Were you really young?"

"No. We were like thirteen."

"And do you remember how we danced?" asks Rodolfo. "I

looked like I was wearing a cast and Tonchi looked like he was trying to start a motorcycle."

They make as if they are wearing full-body casts, dancing a horrible malambo, clownish, moving their arms exaggerat-edly, wearing huge, fake, painted-on smiles. When they finish they sit back down, dying with laughter.

"Oh, dude, you're going to kill me," says Tonchi, wiping his eyes.

Tonchi was born with a congenital kidney disease. He has received two transplants and is on a waiting list for a third. He has to undergo dialysis three times a week, from noon to four in the afternoon. Before and after the dialysis, he goes to the gym, runs, takes malambo classes.

"Dialysis is from twelve to four, and that's it. If you start with 'Oh, poor me, I have to go to dialysis,' you're finished. Now my kidney function is getting worse and worse. Luckily I can uri-nate every morning. It's just a little bit, but I urinate. There are people who between one dialysis and the next don't urinate at all. It helps that I sweat a lot when I dance. But I don't pay much attention to the illness. Last year I had a horrible pain in my abdomen when I was running in Bariloche. An unbe-lievable pain, but I didn't know what was wrong with me. And they were about to operate to remove my appendix when Rodo called me, and I told him, 'Rodo, I'm down here and they're about to take my appendix out.' And Rodo said, 'No, Pa, you don't have an appendix. They removed it when you were little.' So I told the doctor, 'Look, doc, they're telling me here that I don't have an appendix.' I don't know anything about illnesses."

Tonchi's right arm looks like a tree root, full of bulbs

and protuberances, a result of the dialysis. Before coming to Laborde, he underwent a preventive treatment with diuretics to make up for the sessions he'll have to skip while he's away.

"Last year I didn't come, but this year I couldn't let Rodo down. Right, Rodo?"

"Yes, Tonchi, buddy."

Rodolfo can't stop looking at his phone out of the corner of his eye. At noon, we hear steps coming up the side entrance to the house. We all turn and wait expectantly until the face of a young man appears, a beard tracing the outline of his jaw.

"Hello, hello."

"Hey, Freddy," says Rodolfo. "Sit down, *negro*."

Freddy Vacca won the title in 1996, for the province of Tucumán, and he says he's come to say hello and offer his support.

"Do they know yet?"

"No, nothing yet."

They chat about Tuesday's storm, the retirement home where many are staying, the cafeteria, the *peña*, the heat, the power outage, the drought. The conversation strategically avoids anything related to the competition. It seems to be, like so many things here, an unspoken rule. After a while, Vacca stands up and says, "Well, Rodo, I wish you the best. And remember that I'm right there with you, dancing inside of you."

Rodolfo hugs him, thanks him for coming, and Freddy Vacca leaves.

"A king, Freddy."

At twelve thirty nothing's changed: no one calls. Rodolfo

suggests they go to the campground, where his parents are having a barbecue.

"We'll find out while we're there, for sure."

"Rodo, before we go, will you peel me a peach?"

"Sure, Pa, I'll do it right now."

Tonchi loves peaches, but he's allergic to the skin. While Rodolfo peels a peach inside the house, I hear someone ask him, "Hey, Rodo, how are you?"

"Nervous."

————————

In the car on the way to the campground, Rodolfo says, "I thought it would be like last year, that by twelve o'clock we'd know who was going to the finals."

When we get to the highway the phone rings and Rodolfo answers with a firm yet urgent voice:

"Yes, hello."

It's Carlos, Miriam's father.

"No, Carlitos, nothing yet."

The campground looks like a set designed for a happy scene in a movie. The pool is filled with children, smoke rises from the grills. Rodolfo lifts up his nieces and nephews, greets his siblings, his parents. At one p.m. I send a message to Cecilia Lorenc Valcarce: "Anything?" She responds: "Nothing yet."

————————

"I'm really nervous."

Rodolfo sits on a bench, and with the tone of someone confessing their sins, speaking quietly so that his parents don't hear him, he repeats, "Really nervous."

Then we hear a vibration. Rodolfo puts his hand in his pocket, takes out his phone, looks at it, and says, "A message from José Luis Furriol."

José Luis Furriol is the delegate from La Pampa. It's 1:40 in the afternoon.

———————————

And what's going to happen now?
How will it all end?
Will it all end now?

———————————

In the time that passes between the moment Rodolfo receives the message and the moment he reads it, my recorder registers an enormous silence, as if the universe stopped to contemplate the way a few words could determine a man's fate.

Rodolfo opens the message, reads it, and in a clear, modest tone, says, "I'm in the finals."

His mother screams, Miriam screams, his brother and sister scream, the entire campground screams, and from all around we hear, "Let's go, Rodo!" and "Come on, La Pampa!" I never saw the message from José Luis Furriol, because Rodolfo later lost the phone, but it read, "Rodolfo, you're in the finals." While everyone shouts and hugs, I call Cecilia Lorenc Valcarce to get the names of the other finalists. She tells me that he will be up against the hopeful from Río Negro, Maximiliano Castillo, and the hopeful from Santiago del Estero, Sebastián Sayago. Sebastián Sayago: the brother of Fernando Castro, who in turn is the coach and guitar player for Rodolfo, etc.

After a while I say good-bye. We agree that I'll pick Rodolfo up at eleven p.m. to take him to the field. As I walk to the car, I feel privileged: I'm the one who will pick him up. Me.

Am I beginning, maybe, to understand all of this?

———————

That night when I get back to the house, Miriam and Fernando Castro are there too. The mood is somber: in this town where nothing ever happens, Carlos Medina and some of the others staying there had money and jackets stolen out of their truck. The hypothesis is that it was "foreigners," meaning people who aren't from Laborde. Here, like everywhere in the world, the blame is placed on others, outsiders, strangers. In the car, Rodolfo, Miriam, and Fernando are silent, they don't say a word, and I feel like I'm taking a man to the gallows.

We find a parking spot on the dirt road outside the field. As we enter, the Chilean team is dancing onstage. It's still early but we head to the dressing rooms anyway. Rodolfo goes into room number 2. Then everything repeats identically, as if in a recurring dream: he takes a bottle of water out of his brown bag, his sash, his *rastra*, he undresses, he gets dressed, he wets his hair, begins to pace like a rabid, caged tiger, he takes out the Bible, opens it, reads, whispers, closes it, kisses it, puts it away, plays the song "Be You" by Almafuerte on his phone.

It's twelve thirty a.m.

How many times can a man go through this?

How many times can I go through this?

Could this be a story that never ends?

The field is packed. The Argentinian flag waves, high in the sky. Rodolfo is in the dressing room, staring at the floor. Miriam approaches him, hugs him, and without a word, leaves. A few meters away, Sebastián Sayago, dressed in his northern attire, stands in front of the mirror saying, "Come on, come on, come on." At two in the morning the Laborde hymn starts to play, and as soon as it's finished come the fireworks. Over the fireworks, the voice of the announcer:

"Ladies and gentlemen, people of Laborde, the nation! This is the moment of truth, this is the moment we've all been waiting for! This is the reason we've all come here! And only one will become the champion! Ladies and gentlemen, the main malambo category! The competition begins, in this final round ...!"

He breathes in and continues.

"*From Laaa Paaampaaa … Rooodolfooo Gonzáaalez Aaalcán-
tara!*"

There he goes.

The woman's voice, distant, indifferent, says, "Time employed:
four minutes, forty-nine seconds."

Rodolfo exits the stage. He has blood on his toes, his knuck-
les are scraped, there's a cut on his foot. A journalist pounces
for an interview as, onstage, Sebastián Sayago dances. It's 2:20
in the morning. The only thing left to do now is wait.

Rodolfo puts on a jacket—he's wet and it's very cold—
and he goes to see his family. Afterward I find out that they
couldn't all come because they didn't have enough money for
everyone's tickets.

At four a.m. Rodolfo asks Javier, his brother-in-law, to please
go buy him an *alfajor* cookie, because he hasn't eaten one in a
year and a half. At four fifteen he needs to pee, and he has to
take off part of his outfit to go to the bathroom. At four thirty
he returns, gets dressed again, sits in the doorway of the dressing room with his jacket over his shoulders, and eats the two
alfajores that Javier bought him. The hopeful from Río Negro

is locked away in his cubicle, Sebastián Sayago in his. Miriam makes plans on her cell phone to get a strategic seat for the award ceremony. Tonchi stays curled up under the dressing room's cement counter, contemplating the world from that position as if he were very afraid. Rodolfo finishes his *alfajor* and goes in. He sits in a chair, and I sit across from him on an overturned beer crate. In his right hand he has a picture of the Sacred Heart, but I don't know where he got it. Tonchi makes jokes, asks him if he remembers when they were kids and they didn't want to take their naps. Rodolfo nods, laughs, makes an effort to speak.

"Are you nervous?" I ask him after a while.

Rodolfo nods yes, hiding the gesture so that Tonchi doesn't see.

————————

At five in the morning the audience begins to arrive wrapped in blankets to guard against the early-morning cold. But in the dressing room, Rodolfo sweats. The announcer has started to give out the prizes. He asks the representatives from each province to join him onstage. The ceremony is slow because they give out first-, second-, and third-place prizes for every category and sometimes an honorable mention as well. At five fifteen the day starts to brighten. At five thirty the announcer says, "And now, ladies and gentlemen, the main malambo category!"

Rodolfo, sitting in the corner, doesn't say a word. Tonchi,

sitting under the cement table, doesn't say a word. Sitting on the plastic crate, I don't say a word.

"First we'll announce the runner-up for this year. Ladies and gentlemen, the runner-up for this year, the forty-fifth edition of the most Argentinian of all festivals, is from the province *ooooof...!*"

The announcer breathes in, and with an exhale, says:

"*Santiaaaaagooo del Eeeeesteroooooo! Sebastiáaan Sayaaaaaago!*"

I peek out and see Sebastián Sayago walking to the stage. He doesn't look very happy, and many of the people with him are crying. Another year, I say to myself. Another year of twelve malambos a day, an hour of jogging. Another year of terrible hope.

Rodolfo stands, and with the picture of the Sacred Heart in his hand, he turns his back to me and prays.

The announcer invites Gonzalo "Pony" Molina to the stage for his last malambo. Pony dances—a dance I don't see—and when he finishes he goes up to the microphone and speaks about his friends, his family, his eternal gratitude. His words are muffled by emotion and by the improper distance between his mouth and the microphone.

Rodolfo stops praying, puts on his hat, and leaves the dressing room. Outside are Miriam, Carlos Medina, and Fernando Castro: they all look like they're trying to survive a natural disaster. As if Rodolfo were made of some very fragile material, no one approaches him, no one speaks to him.

The announcer says, "Ladies and gentlemen ... now for the name you've all been waiting to hear, the name of our champion!"

Rodolfo walks in circles. Miriam leans against a wall and looks at him as if she wants to shout at him or burst out crying. Tonchi peeks out from the doorway of the dressing room.

"The judges of this year's festival extend the title of national malambo champion tooo ... !"

Then the name of the champion bursts forth and this is the first thing that happens: Tonchi and Rodolfo hug and fall to their knees. Tonchi cries uncontrollably and Rodolfo doesn't let go of him, but he doesn't cry. He closes his eyes tightly, as if he's just been punched.

Fireworks explode over the stage, and at the center of the universe stand these two men, this small nucleus of unconditional friendship that pulses with the heartbeat of all the hungry winters and Tonchi's shattered kidneys and Rodolfo's busted sneakers, because the announcer has just said that the new champion at Laborde, ladies and gentlemen, is him, is Rodolfo González Alcántara, and Miriam covers her mouth with her hands and starts to cry, and Carlos Medina cries, and Fernando Castro cries, and Rodolfo and Tonchi stay there, kneeling, until Miriam goes over and Rodolfo stands up and hugs her, and Fernando Castro goes over and Rodolfo hugs him, and the Laborde hymn plays over the voice of the announcer who asks, "Where is the champion? Where is the champion?"

Carlos Medina dries his eyes and says, "Rodo, Rodo, you have to go onstage!"

Rodolfo runs a hand through his hair, straightens his hat, and goes onstage. And the first thing he does, before taking the trophy from Pony's hands, is hug the runner-up, Sebastián Sayago.

That's it, I tell myself.

There goes a man whose life has changed forever.

No more sliding under the turnstiles.

No more worn-out sneakers.

No more hunger.

———————

Pony hands Rodolfo the trophy and he raises it over his head, sets it on the floor, throws his hands up, and makes the sign of the cross. The announcer says, "An amazing award ceremony, just after five thirty in the morning! Now we're going to let the national malambo champion dance! Ladies and gentlemen, dancing as the 2012 national malambo champion: Rodolfo González Alcántara!"

As tradition dictates, Rodolfo dances a few figures of his first malambo as champion, one of the last malambos of his life. Then he goes to the microphone and with a firm voice, without a hint of emotion, says:

"Hello. What I want is to give thanks. Thanks to my family, because they did something incredible. Since they couldn't afford to stay in the campground, in order to come, they rented a bus for forty-five people, which was cheaper, and when they get home they're going to have to work a lot to pay back the money. To all my teachers. To the friends I've made along the way. And to the woman I chose, to Miriam. Because we malambo dancers have to work hard, but the real sacrifice is made by those who support us: they support a dream that doesn't even belong to them. So thanks to all of you."

It's five forty-five in the morning on the first day of the rest of his life.

———————

A year later, Saturday, January 12, 2013, the first thing you see when you arrive in Laborde is a gigantic photo of Rodolfo. When you turn the corner, another. And then another. And another. His feet, his hands, his waist, his face, his torso—his entire body is scattered around the town as if in an act of crazed dismemberment. It's six in the evening, and in the pressroom on the field an open conversation between the champion and the public is just ending. Wearing a sweater and jeans—the cuffs rolled up—Rodolfo signs autographs on small posters bearing his photo. Every autograph takes him a long time, because he asks everyone for the exact spelling of their names and then writes a long dedication. He told me he's having trouble sleeping and doesn't like to think about his final malambo, which he'll dance on Monday.

Walking around Laborde with him is impossible. An entire team of soccer players out jogging shouts at him: "Rodolfo González Alcántara, stallion!" People ask him for photos, autographs, hugs. He smiles, says hello, he's patient, friendly, shy: when the owner of the Riccione ice cream parlor asks him to top by and pick up a huge banner with his picture that she wants to give him, Rodolfo, who's dressed as a gaucho, asks me to go with him, because he's embarrassed to walk around dressed like that outside the field.

All through 2012, Rodolfo's life changes dramatically. Not only does he have more work—as a judge at other festivals, as an instructor—but his wages have increased considerably. Finding himself with an amount of money he never thought he'd see, he built a studio for classes in his house in Pablo Podestá. In time he'll probably be able to give up the classes around Greater Buenos Aires and focus only on his classes at the IUNA and the students who come to his home.

It's almost eight p.m., but the sun is still out and we're in the car, on a dirt road, parked in front of a cemetery, looking out over a field of soy that was full of corn last year. I ask him if he's still training.

"Yes, I was just in Santa Rosa running out on the dunes. But it's really hard to train without any objective. When I trained to come to Laborde, I would think that somewhere else in the country, at that exact moment, there was a hopeful practicing his malambo ten times a day. So I practiced mine twelve times. Or that there was some hopeful out there who at that same moment was jogging an hour a day. So I jogged an hour and a half. If you don't have a reason, it's really hard to keep up that pace."

"And was winning the title as great as you thought it would be?"

"It was so much more. They idolize you. This past week here, I've felt like a king. I know that as long as I live, I'll never again feel like I did this week in Laborde. But after Monday, someone else is going to take all that attention."

That night we go to the field early, because Rodolfo has been coaching one of his students, Álvaro Melián, who will compete at nine thirty in the special youth category. Rodolfo says that if Álvaro wins in his category and Sebastián Sayago takes the title of champion, it would be a perfect ending. Rumor has it that Sebastián danced a good malambo, but they also say that he never fully recovered from his injury in 2012. If he makes it to the finals, he'll have to dance in a lot of pain.

"To close out my championship with those two things would be a dream," says Rodolfo as we walk toward the dressing rooms. "Sebas deserves it. He's a very simple and humble guy. I hope he wins, with all my heart."

This year, the dressing room area has been painted white and there are signs with black lettering: DRESSING ROOM 1, DRESSING ROOM 2. A little girl dressed as a *paisana* comes up to ask Rodolfo for an autograph, and Rodolfo asks her if she can wait a minute because his hopeful is about to go on.

"Of course. You're the champion for the rest of your life," says the girl.

Rodolfo smiles at her and pats her head. He walks to the edge of the stage ,and as Álvaro begins to dance, I watch him do something I've seen him do so many times: he makes the sign of the cross.

———————

At two on Sunday afternoon the finalists for the main malambo are announced: Rodrigo Heredia, for Córdoba; Ariel Pérez, for

Buenos Aires; and Sebastián Sayago, for Santiago del Estero. Álvaro Melián, Rodolfo's student, has also made it to the finals for his category.

At three in the morning on Monday, Rodolfo is in the press-room. He's dressed in his northern-style clothing and he has a stuffy nose.

"I think it's because I slept with the air conditioner on."

Since the start of the festival on Tuesday, he's gone onstage many times to dance *zamba*, the waltz, a *cueca*. Active participation during the following year's festival is an important part of the agreement with the reigning champion, and it includes, in addition to some exchange trips to Chile, Bolivia, and Paraguay, malambo workshops in Laborde that they give free of charge.

The three hopefuls for the main category have already danced. Sebastián Sayago, in spite of his injury, danced a northern malambo that was luxurious, exasperating, dramatic, an onslaught that left Fernando Castro, who watched from the audience, crying his eyes out.

"He did what he had to do; he didn't leave any doubts. But we'll have to wait and see," says Rodolfo.

Miriam chats with her parents, who've come up from Patagonia. Fernando Castro, who's now moved north to Salta to work as an instructor for a folkloric dance company, tunes his guitar. He looks impeccable in his jeans and dress shirt. Rodolfo puts drops in his nose, poses for a photo with the mayor of Laborde. I think back to last year at this time: Tonchi had taken cover under the counter in dressing room 2 as if he were expecting a gale-force wind, and Rodolfo was coping with his anxiety by praying to a little picture of the Sacred Heart.

At four in the morning, Rodolfo gets dressed in his southern-style clothing and practices his malambo in front of the mirror. At four thirty we head to the stage.

———————

The award ceremony is, once again, long and slow. By five thirty we know that Álvaro Melián did not win his category and that the runner-up for the main malambo is Ariel Pérez, from the province of Buenos Aires. The announcer then states that the time has come to say good-bye to the 2012 champion.

"The country has gathered here in the national malambo capital, and we're now in the final stretch of this emotional forty-sixth edition! Now, here to dance for us, Rodolfo González Alcántara, from the province of La Pampa, the 2012 champion, who for the last year has received the admiration of the entire country! And a champion says good-bye with a dance, before the people of the most Argentinian of all festivals!"

Rodolfo, who waits between the curtains on the side of the stage, makes the sign of the cross and goes out. From the audience come shouts of "Let's go, Rodo!" and "Come on, champ!"

It's five forty-five in the morning.

It's five fifty when he finishes dancing the last malambo of his life and the crowd's applause descends upon him. He kisses the stage, stands back up, walks to the microphone, and says:

"It's hard to be here. I could have just kept on dancing forever. But my body has had it. Today I woke up kind of sad, I really felt like crying, because this is the end of my career.

Laborde gave me everything, and today it's taking everything. Everything stays here. I hope to be able to represent Laborde and our country as perfectly as possible. To everyone who comes here. To everyone who dreams. Thank you, people of Laborde, for making me feel like a king. For giving me so much. For helping me become what I am."

The audience shouts, Rodolfo raises his arms to the sky and gives thanks. Then he backs away and stands off to one side.

The announcer says, "Ladies and gentlemen, now we will present none other than the new national malambo champion …!"

The first rays of sun climb up the sky, blocked only by the traces of a few red clouds. A cold tension spreads over the audience.

"Laborde tells the people of Argentina and the world, on this new day that's just dawned, the name of the champion! Of their forty-sixth champion! Ladies and gentlemen! The 2013 national malambo champion is from the province *ooooooof…* *Santiaaa…!*"

Before he can say *Santiago del Estero*, before he can say *Sebastián Sayago*, the crowd explodes. Backstage, Sebastián, in a confusion of embraces, cries. From the other side of the stage Rodolfo looks at me, smiles, clenches his fist, and raises it in a gesture of triumph. Without even thinking about it, I respond with the same gesture. Sebastián comes onstage, hugs Rodolfo, takes the trophy, and as he dances his first malambo as champion—one of the last malambos of his life—Rodolfo discreetly descends the stairs at the edge of the stage. There, leaning on a low wall, Miriam waits for him. He hugs her, his feet covered in blood. She cries, but he doesn't say a word. A little boy comes up and taps him on the shoulder.

"Champ, can you give me your autograph?"

Rodolfo breaks away from the embrace and looks at him. The boy must be around eight years old and he wears his hair long, like all malambo dancers.

"For my little friend, of course. Where do you want me to sign?"

The boy, pointing to his back, says, "My shirt."

Rodolfo bends down and, with considerable effort, writes a message on the boy's back. Then he says good-bye, walks to the pressroom, and in a corner begins to get undressed. He takes off his jacket, his *rastra*, his sash, his shirt. And before putting it all away in his brown bag, he gives each item a kiss.

I didn't see him cry, but he cried.

ACKNOWLEDGMENT

A special thanks to Cecilia Lorenc Valcarce
for her help and support.

New Directions Paperbooks — a partial listing

*BILINGUAL EDITION

For a complete listing, request a free catalog from New Directions, 80 8th Avenue, New York, NY 10011
or visit us online at **ndbooks.com**